FREEING YOUR INTUITION

 a beginner's guide

GW00691109

GILLIAN STOKES

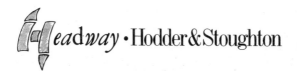eadway · Hodder&Stoughton

Thanks to
James Pollicott
for his original ideas for the
illustrations for this book

Order queries: please contact Bookpoint Ltd, 39 Milton Park, Abingdon, Oxon OX14
4TD. Telephone: (44) 01235 400414, Fax: (44) 01235 400454. Lines are open from
9.00 - 6.00, Monday to Saturday, with a 24 hour message answering service. Email
address: orders@bookpoint.co.uk

A catalogue record for this title is available from the British Library.

ISBN 0 340 71149 3

First published 1998
Impression number 10 9 8 7 6 5 4 3 2 1
Year   2003 2002 2001 1999 1998

Copyright © 1998 Gillian Stokes

Typeset by Transet Limited, Coventry, England.
Printed in Great Britain for Hodder & Stoughton Educational, a division of Hodder
Headline plc, 338 Euston Road, London NW1 3BH by Cox and Wyman Limited,
Reading, Berks.

CONTENTS

INTRODUCTION

A moment's insight is sometimes worth a life's experience.

Oliver Wendell Holmes (1809–94)

Could you do with some good advice and wise counsel? Do you value your intuition? Take guidance from the person who knows you best: yourself. With wiser decisions you can make your own luck, increase your creativity and improve performance in all areas of your life. Intuition is a natural faculty that we all possess, though we may perceive it in various ways. You can learn how to identify and enhance your intuition, and make your intuition work for you. Learn to recognise what you know, not just what you think.

What could a mental experience be if it does not involve reason? To our minds, so steeped in the ideas of rational science, it is hard to credit that there could be any such thing. Scientific enquiry demands that facts be replicable, verifiable and reasonable. To the traditional scientific mind therefore, any claim for an experience involving unreasoned perception must be an irrational fantasy. Intuition, with its spontaneous and individual nature, cannot conform to scientific evaluation, but this should not demean its worth. Intuition is as valuable a talent as the ability to reason or analyse. Those scientists and philosophers who would deny the existence of intuition, choose to forget that most of the great scientific advances of the past followed from the spontaneous intuition of their discoverers. If scientific progress is to continue to be expanded by further generations, it is vital that there should be a reappraisal of the role and importance of intuition in creativity. Rationality and the dominance of science has historically devalued

1

intuition and subjectivity, yet ironically, it is now modern science and logic which is leading the change in such narrow-minded attitudes.

Thankfully, we do not have to be a genius to benefit from intuitive wisdom. It can be a helpful resource in all our endeavours and bring a significant benefit at personal, social and global levels. *Freeing your Intuition* describes how you can discover, develop and encourage this very practical skill to your benefit and that of those around you.

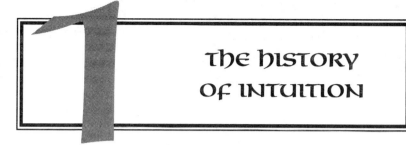

tbe bistory of intuition

If reason and empirical observation steer the course of discovery and the passion for truth supplies the fuel, it is intuition that provides the spark.

Philip Goldberg, *The Intuitive Edge*, 1983

The dominant western philosophical tradition, of modern times, favours reason and thinking at the expense of being and knowing. It was not always so. Intuition was once regarded as a glimpse into an eternal wisdom, a realm which affects us, but which we have no direct access to. In this chapter we will look at some historical precedents, including ideas expressed by the philosopher Plato, and the psychologist, Carl Jung.

Plato and Ancient Greece

The Greek philosopher, Plato, (inspired by his teacher, Socrates) considered our tangible world to be but a poor reflection of a *real* world which was too magnificent for our limited human senses to comprehend. In his famous analogy, *The Cave*, he describes what we know as real via our senses, as being like shadows cast upon a cave wall by a fire behind us, which we cannot see. We are like prisoners, Plato continues, chained in such a way that we cannot turn and see the truth of our situation, and the limitation of what we take to be reality. Anyone who would escape this imprisonment and see the magnificence of the reality beyond the cave could never more be

satisfied with mere reflections on a cave wall, but neither could such a person convince the remaining prisoners that what they see is only a dim reflection of a greater reality. In other words, you had to have been there.

Plato's Cave

Plato/Socrates also proposed a *theory of forms*. Plato's *forms* can be thought of as perfect prototypes for every item on earth. These ideal models or patterns dictate the form that earthly objects will take. Plato goes on to suggest we have a forgotten memory of the perfect *forms* which remains within from when we dwelt among them before our own birth. When born here, he says, we forget what we knew of that perfection, yet deep within us lies the memory which can be reactivated. When we seem to learn, says Plato, we merely remember what we once knew, since in the realm of *forms*, all that could ever be, already exists.

If we can accept such ideas as the *forms*, or the idea that our reality is a lesser illusion of a greater truth, we can suppose that when we experience intuition, we are receiving information from this sort of metaphysical energy field, or pool of collective consciousness, wherein all is timeless, and already known.

The Middle Ages

The Middle Ages was a turning point for intuitive wisdom. The advent of printing resulted in the gradual increase and availability of knowledge as proclaimed by others. Formerly it was normal to rely on direct sensation and knowledge gained from personal contact, or experience with objects, people and ideas. Printing marked the beginning of a shift in trust and reliance towards words, symbols and images rather than on immediate personal contact.

The new emphasis on learned ideas and abstract knowledge prepared the way for later scientific developments, which would seem to offer solutions to all our questions about the world around us. The printed word was first the property of an elite class of monks and scholars, who gained power over those who could not read. This elite had an advantage as the laws governing property and inheritance, religious observance and scientific wisdom became ever increasingly available in this new format.

Gradually reliance upon the information conveyed by the written word replaced direct perception and immediate knowledge, which as a result became devalued. Intuition became less trusted since it could not be shared by others, except as an unverifiable report. Not surprisingly, intuition fell from favour, since it offers no traces of the pathways by which its conclusions are arrived at, and therefore cannot be replicated or traced by others. Mystical religious experiences and revelations continued to be valued for a time, and were even printed. Mystics were perceived as extraordinary anyway, so for a while their intuitions continued to be valued as a special case.

However in time, even this source of intuitive authority was subject to doubt. As reading became nearly universal, scientific methods became dominant, and personal experience was devalued, however sacred its source.

The Age of Reason

From the eighteenth century onwards, the scientific age offered anyone the opportunity to read how conclusions were reached, and to recreate the experiments which led to the conclusions drawn; assuming the means and intelligence. Reliance on the power of reason to determine reality was paramount at this time. Science and philosophy favoured logical and rational approaches to problems. Methods should be systematic and accurate, follow objective principles and work towards the collection of an exact body of knowledge. Theories collectively subscribed to could not now successfully be questioned by the subjective intuition of a lone dissident. There was a return to a valuing of the individual, but now as a reasoning being. Religion and intuition became devalued and together with mystical phenomena, were increasingly seen as the product of misguided minds.

It is not surprising, therefore, that intuition, which does not reveal how it works, should have become mistrusted and cast aside. However, the scientific method has been found to have its limitations, too. With the advent of new technologies, modern physics and logic, some aspects of intuition are finding favour again today.

Intuition and Carl Jung

The notion that we have an inner life, as well as our momentary outer experiences and behaviour, was as radical a shift in commonplace belief in the nineteenth century as the emphasis on rationality had been in the century before. It is hard to imagine now a time when there was no conception of terms such as *unconscious*,

instinctive drives and *archetypes,* or before it was thought that experiences in childhood might have a bearing on our adult lives. These assumptions are now so commonplace for most people, that our very language and thinking are shaped by them.

The Swiss psychologist, Carl Jung (1875–1961) describes what he calls *archetypes*. These are a similar idea in some respects to Plato's *forms*. In both theories we can only know the ideal *form* or *archetype* through their earthly copies, because human sense limitations prevent us comprehending the limitless potential of the originals. Jung's *archetypes* remain beyond our mental grasp as something like an all-potential energy with no material existence. It may help to imagine a core spirit which unites all individual examples of the one idea, though each idea or image is separately and individually interpreted by us. So, for example, we may each have our own image of the *archetype* MOTHER, which have at the core, a similar understanding of what mother-ness typically is, but which we each cloak with particular meaning and images, according to our culture and personal experiences. Thus according to Jung, the same *archetype* may trigger many myths and images, and according to Plato; every individual object will have a corresponding, perfect but intangible, *form*.

This notion of a reality greater than that of our common perception is appealing, though direct knowledge is not sufficient proof of such a fabulous realm. It may be that Plato used simple stories and parables to explain a more abstract idea; a level of consciousness available to us, but rarely tapped. The idea of a finer and wiser place from which we are now excluded, like the Garden of Eden, is itself a popular and common *archetype* in many cultures.

Personality types

Jung also proposed a model of human consciousness involving four basic *personality types*. Each type has a paired opposite, and will reveal the preferred way we use our mind, both to perceive reality and to judge what we perceived. Whichever personality type we

prefer to use governs how we perceive the world around us, the judgements we make, and what we do about what we see. We will inevitably be better at using whichever of the mind-types we favour, simply by virtue of accumulated experience and expertise. This then re-emphasises that choice, since most of us prefer to do whatever we are best at.

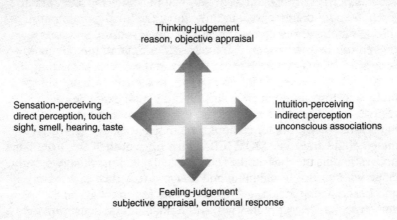

Thinking-judgement
reason, objective appraisal

Sensation-perceiving
direct perception, touch
sight, smell, hearing, taste

Intuition-perceiving
indirect perception
unconscious associations

Feeling-judgement
subjective appraisal, emotional response

Jung's four personality types (as paired opposites)

Jung recognised intuition as one of these four personality types; each of them a natural and basic aspect of consciousness. Accordingly, he grouped some of the types as natural opposites; the person who predominantly functions by favouring thought and reason, would be quite different from one for whom feelings and emotions are their primary interpretation of reality. Similarly someone who favours the physical senses would be quite different from the person who relies on hunches, and who intuits the possibilities in a situation, reading cues and sensing underlying situations.

The *sensation-perceiver* will tend to ignore hints in favour of what the senses report to be the case. If your preferred way of perceiving with your mind involves more reliance on your senses, you will tend to pay little or no attention to the hints, hunches and possibilities in a situation, all of which the intuitive type of personality will be more attuned to. For the sense-perceiver, an intelligent person is one who

draws valid conclusions from solid facts, who prefers routines, and who is good with details.

Jung describes intuition as an indirect perception by way of the unconscious. The *intuitive-perceiver* is thus always seeking and perceiving hints and subtleties which this type regards as more significant than information detected via the senses. The personality which favours intuition may well neglect the actual situation around them, so absorbed are they in following perceived hints and clues. On the other hand, this type may pick up nuances which the sensation type would miss entirely. If intuition dominates the unconscious, the individual tends to interpret life according to mystical and symbolic ideals which can set them apart from the experiences of the mundane everyday life of other types. The *intuitive* type can be a source of inspiration to others. Their ability to sense the potential and direction in a situation, and to read cues from other people, makes them great innovators and evaluators. However, the *intuitive's* need for constant stimulation and new challenges can make them seem unreliable. For the *intuition-perceiver*, an intelligent person is one who can foresee trends and act on them, who creates change, and who is good with the broader picture.

The remaining two pairs of personality types, *thinking/judging* and *feeling/judging*, between them govern the way we prefer to *judge* what we *perceived* with the previous pair. Some people prefer to rely primarily upon thinking processes in judging the truth of their perceptions, while others will rely on their feelings and emotions as the most reliable measure of a situation.

By the time we are adult, whichever are the less favoured pair of personality types may have slipped from our consciousness altogether, into our unconscious where it still has some influence, but in ways beyond conscious control. Whichever personality type predominates in consciousness will have the opposite of the pair predominating in the unconscious. As the term suggests, the unconscious is just that, beyond our knowing, so we will be quite unaware that the inferior function type holds sway over our unconscious reactions, unless we begin to suspect a pattern with particular aspects of our life. To give an example, the *thinking* type

9

would not find that the expression of feelings comes easily, just as the *feeling* type would have difficulty with analytical, logical thought processes. This would help to explain how some people seem to have easy access to their intuitive processes whereas for others it requires the adoption of techniques to enable this repressed function to flourish.

Of course, Jung says, we all exhibit some aspects of all these types; no one is exclusively one type; but the defining personality characteristic will be which pair we favour over the others. Whichever function we favour in our interactions with the world colours our judgements, and our preferred mode of judgement influences what we will perceive. So, as we filter our experience through our favoured mode, we shape both the world we perceive and our reactions to it. Frequent use improves the reliability of the chosen way of relating, as we act, so we become, which leads to the dominance of one pair. No type can be said to be right or wrong either. Each has its value, but the person who can bring a degree of balance between the different ways of using their mind will have an advantage over those who ignore or deny some aspects. Any latent capacity can be developed and strengthened, even if not our favoured choice. Employers would do well to match their employees' favoured personality types to the corporate aspirations, and employ each person where their type of personality will do the most good.

PRACTICE

1 What are the four main personality types described by Carl Jung?
2 What perception type do you believe you are?
3 Which development in the Middle Ages, lessened the value attributed to individual experience and intuition?
4 Plato's cave dwelling prisoners could not believe tales of the wider world brought to them by those who had escaped the cave. Why?

wbaT is
iNTUiTiON?

*As to what happens when I compose,
I really haven't the faintest idea.*

Samuel Barber (1910–81)

Everyone will have their own answer to the question, 'What is intuition?' Some people describe intuition as a hunch or a gut feeling, some experience it as a sudden flash of certainty or inspiration, while to others it seems as though they have been granted a revelation. In some cases you may be able to trace the origins of the information which now flashes into your mind, while in others there are no known links whatever. Who can say what is intuition and what is premonition? You may have a strong reaction on meeting someone for the first time, though you have no prior information about them. This judgement is a form of psychic intuition. You may not choose to become a psychic, but you can develop your receptivity to intuitions. True psychics experience intuitive revelations on a regular basis and some claim to tune in to them at will. Most people, however, will experience at least a few intuitive revelations during their life. You may hear an inner voice, or feel a physical vibration in your body, accompanied by a sense of intense clarity. On occasions this intensity can cause physiological reactions similar to excitement or anxiety, such is the certainty with which you feel the rightness, or wrongness of an act or an interpretation.

These experiences have all been noted as accompanying intuitive experiences but they do not define them. Definitions apply rigid categories, but intuition, as a dynamic process rather than a tangible

thing, will always be more than the labels we can attach to it. You may experience none of the phenomena I have mentioned yet still be the recipient of accurate intuitional states. One thing is clear, intuition, however defined, is essentially experienced in a personal way and is always recognised as an inner experience.

Whatever may be said to come from our unconscious, by definition is exactly that, beyond conscious awareness, and will therefore be unknown until such time as it becomes conscious and known by us. Intuition presents an individual with enlightenment via the insight of new meaning. It transcends the usual divisions of knower and known, me and you. Since intuition expands knowledge by the process of gaining new meaning, it follows that intuition is the product of a particular mind in relation to its situation, or of a particular mind's conscious attempts to solve a problem. For this reason no one else can experience exactly the same intuition as you, although rarely, other people may simultaneously have an intuition which leads them to the same conclusion. These normally unique and unreplicable properties make it difficult to generalise about intuition. Difficult, but not impossible.

Take a moment now to consider how and when you experience intuition. One factor common to intuitive experiences, when clearly perceived, and correctly interpreted, is that they prove to be right. We just know, without any doubt, that what is intuited will come about, when we feel that spontaneous certainty. If asked to explain how we know, we cannot, and being used to the need to account for our decisions, we may then allow doubt to creep in, for fear of seeming foolish. At the moment of an intuitive leap or flash, however, there is absolutely no doubt or need for judgement. There is a beauty and simplicity to intuitive truth which can cause us to marvel at what has been revealed, and wonder how we could previously have missed it. Frequently there is an accompanying sense of urgency, exaltation and honour to be the recipient of such spontaneous certainty. We recognise we are in the presence of truth.

Although not usually given to fears regarding transport, we sometimes have a clear sense that we must not take a particular train or aeroplane. We are the only person who can judge whether we have experienced a genuine intuition, because for good or ill, we

will have to face the consequences. Occasionally we may have a sense of impending danger which defies explanation. If we heed the intuition and change our plans we may never know whether our action was justified, but some individuals have ignored such a warning with tragic consequences. One of the children killed in the disaster at the small Welsh mining village, Aberfan, had a warning dream the previous night. She told her mother about her dream in the morning, but went to school as usual. The school was engulfed by an avalanche of mud and coal waste later that day and the girl was killed along with most of her school friends.

A popular misconception states that intuition is the sole province of one gender, as suggested by the stereotype of *woman's intuition*. Though a recent report does allege a genetic predisposition to intuition in girls, which is thought to be lacking in boys, the jury is still out on that one. However, we employ a form of intuition every day regardless of our gender and do so in such a commonplace way that we do not even consider it intuition. Once we learn the rules of how the world seems to work, which is part of the process of growing up, we learn also that we can trust that some mental processing does not need our conscious attention. There are good evolutionary reasons for why we cannot easily access the contents of our unconscious. Whether we believe the mind is a repository of past information, as dream content would suggest, or merely reflects an ever present awareness; the welter of information which floods our senses could overwhelm us. Intuition, dreams and visions may be glimpses from beyond this necessary barrier.

Every time you make a decision or a judgement you rely on your intuition. Does that seem a crazy statement? When you perform mundane, everyday actions do you stop to gather all the pros and cons, analyse them and then make a logically evaluated decision based on the facts? Of course not. If you were to do so, your senses would be saturated with all the data gathered from your surroundings, which you would then be kept busy consciously evaluating. You would have to consider the wisdom of each single step and the significance of every momentary change in your environment. I am not referring here to occasions where you need to make a big *either/or* call. These will mostly become available to your mind for conscious

choice, nor am I referring to instinctual behaviour. I refer to the amount of petty decisions which occur beyond your conscious awareness at all times.

We act every day without ever stopping to make a conscious judgement and without considering that we do so. A young child, for example, learning to walk or to ride a bicycle, will concentrate consciously on the skills required for balance which will become second nature when the task is mastered. Once we learn to walk or ride a bicycle, unless we become injured or diseased, we will never again not know how to walk or ride, nor will we give either act much thought. This reliance on acquired, preconscious automatic functioning is an example of how we could learn to trust in our intuition once we become sufficiently assured of its wisdom.

Although intuition has on occasion been a spur to world shattering discoveries made by scientific and mathematical geniuses it is also the province of each of us leading a less exalted life. Where people do differ is in the degree of trust and reliance they place upon this valuable resource. If you have been taught to value reason above all else, this trust may be minimal even when in everyday activities you are unconsciously relying on intuition all the time. The best that we can do is observe the times and situations under which it has occurred in the past, and hope that by replicating these we may be fortunate.

Where does intuition come from?

The short answer is that no one knows. Few of us can explain the intricacies of a central heating system either, but we settle for the fact that it works, if it does. I will briefly explore some possibilities, but the debate about potential levels of consciousness and being beyond that which we experience everyday is beyond the scope of this book.

Inspiration descends only in flashes, to clothe circumstances, it is not stored up in a barrel, like salt herrings, to be doled out.

Patrick White (1912–90) *Voss* 1957

No self

Perhaps the very sense of ourselves as separate, individual beings is mistaken, as many world faiths suggest. Buddhists hold as a basic truth, the notion that we have of a *self* is an illusion. Mystics from all parts of the world, and of all religions describe experiences of the oneness of all life. If what we take to be our separate identity is illusory, we would be freed from the need to assume that *we* occupy a place in the stream of time. Take away the need to assume time as a linear concept along which we have our being, like knots in a piece of string, and we might replace it with other models of existence more compatible with experiences like intuition.

Perhaps what seems to be our identity is no more than a harmonic, a sort of bundle of energy, which though it is temporarily associated with a physical form, only has an apparent identity. Harmonic in this sense does not mean what we might think of as morally good or bad, just consistent, like the vibration of a note from a tuning fork expressing a particular frequency. The particular vibration *we* manifest would then perhaps be determined according to how we behave, and the cluster of energy which that produces. What we believe we experience as identity might be just a temporarily consistent and harmonic collection of experiences, in the soup that is everything.

This may not be as far fetched as it seems at first. After all, we know we change every atom of our physical bodies over time, and our mental body is constantly adapting to new experiences. Just what about you is identical with the *you* of the past? Do you feel you are exactly the person you were at age ten, at age thirty, or even yesterday? We use the convention of speaking of a self because it is convenient and generally accepted practice, but it could be that it misleads.

What effect might the notion of no-self have on the operation of intuition? Well, we know that our focus on a particular issue can attract intuitive experience. With this in mind, perhaps in concentrating on a particular issue we alter our *frequency* temporarily, so that *we* change the frequency at which we vibrate. This would then have the effect of attracting a different set of *frequencies* as though we had re-tuned a radio to a new station. If our energy and commitment creates a match in the *soup* that is everything, we may briefly have a sense of the answer we sought. Similarly psychic experiences may be a brief blip at a reciprocal frequency to that which we currently operate, which stimulates awareness of what we imagine to represent the *future* or events *elsewhere*.

To recap; this model frees us from assuming that we occupy a fixed place in time and space as an identity, though our attendant physicality leads us to suppose otherwise. There would be no sense in speaking of me and you, of I and not I, of now and then. Everything everywhere that is and ever will be would surround and permeate us in a symphony of harmonics. To perceive something from the *future* would then be perceiving something from the ever-present, because in truth, that is all there is. If intuition operates from a ground of limitless potential, this temporary cluster of being (you, me) focused on a particular issue, might serve to attract harmonious information to it. The sense of certainty that something you are already focused on is about to occur may then be because in some sense you have flagged that event, and formed a link with it, or the people connected to it. Perhaps it is enough for the person who knows of your interest to think of you, to alert you when they are in a position to know what you as yet do not.

I once sensed an inexplicable urge to contact someone who, though emotionally close to me, for complicated reasons had been out of my life for years. I felt compelled to write and explain all the reasons why I had not been in touch, together with an explanation of all the misunderstandings that had passed between us many years before. It was important for me to come clean, though I had no idea why. I had no news, and I did not even have a telephone at the time. I learned soon after that my letter had reached the hospital bed where this

person had just been operated upon for cancer. I was relieved that I had cleared the air before learning of the illness, because otherwise it might have seemed I had written as the result of a guilty conscience. But how did I know? The answer is, I didn't. All I did know was that I had to write and tell all, and I acted because the strength of the intuitive feeling demanded it. Similar experiences among those with whom we have an emotionally close bond are far from rare.

What intuition is not

Reaction to an external stimulus, such as a poet moved to write a sonnet after hearing birdsong, is an inspirational influence but not an intuition, because the source of the inspiration is known or can be traced, whereas the source of true intuition remains a mystery. Neither is intuition some sort of fortune telling, amenable to our bidding. If it were, we could control our destiny by deciding which premonitions we would have, and of those, which we would accept and which we would ignore. We could certainly become rich, but if everyone could do likewise, rich and poor would have no meaning because we would all have exactly what we decided to have.

At times your mind finds a new way of interpreting facts which you were already aware of, but had not previously connected in this particular way. You may have picked up cues from your environment without consciously being aware of doing so, then what seems to be intuition is the conscious recognition and patterning of these cues and their transformation into meaningful awareness. Intuition is not merely a guess based on super fast reasoning of perceived hints and cues. We all pick up on subtle signs in other people, for instance, without necessarily knowing that we do so and without that being intuition. When we guess that someone is untrustworthy, for instance, it is more likely to be our learned awareness of the body language and the fidgets associated with telling a lie than a case of intuition. Problems can arise if cues are ignored. It is useful to know that a snarling dog may bite you, but it is not a case of intuition if it does. Reading the environment, including the creatures in it, is a survival technique which some

people have learned better than others. Intuition is more than instinct. A moment's consideration will reveal the truth of this statement. Instinctual behaviours such as the fear of heights or loud noises with which we are born, do not involve conscious awareness, whereas an intuition involves a heightened sense of conscious awareness; quite the opposite of instinct.

Intuition does not respond to the self-deluding demands of wishful thinking either. In science and mathematics many theories have been shattered by the wisdom revealed in a flash of intuition. If wishful thinking could be directed to determine the outcome of an avenue of research there would be a natural tendency among scientists to create only intuitions which support their pet theories, but more often than not, intuition disproves pet theories. Intuition seems to be more than just a creative synthesis of already known facts, though the facts help to create our focus.

The track record

There have been many historically important instances of discoveries, inventions and acts of creativity which owe their existence in some measure to intuition. Perhaps a mention of some of the more famous examples attributed to intuition might help to convince any remaining sceptics. Most of these famous cases confirm the elusive and spontaneous nature of the intuitive experience, but failure to harness intuition is no justification for disputing its credentials.

Intuition in music:

- Johann Sebastian Bach, the great German composer, when asked where he found his melodies, replied that the problem lay not in finding them, but in getting up in the morning and getting out of bed without stepping on them.
- Samuel Barber, composer of the beautiful *Adagio for strings*, is reported to have said, 'As to what happens when I compose, I

really haven't the faintest idea' thus revealing that the process was beyond his rational control.

- Mozart reportedly said of his compositions, '...my subject enlarges itself, becomes methodised and defined, and the whole, though it be long, stands almost complete and finished in my mind, so that I can survey it, like a fine picture or a beautiful statue, at a glance. Nor do I hear in my imagination the parts successively, but I hear them, as it were, all at once....Whence and how they come, I know not, nor can I force them.'
- Peter Tchaikovsky, composer, stated in a letter of 1878 that frequently when in a somnambulist state, 'The germ of a future composition comes suddenly and unexpectedly...It takes root with extraordinary force and rapidity.'

Intuition in poetry:

- A.E. Houseman, author of *The Shropshire Lad*, related how poems would often come to him while shaving. He also described how at other times, when walking along and thinking of nothing in particular '...there would flow into my mind, with sudden and unaccountable emotion, sometimes a line or two of verse, sometimes a whole stanza at once.'
- Stephen Spender, the American poet, wrote an article for *Partisan Review*, 'The Making of a Poem', in which he said, 'Inspiration is the beginning of a poem and also its final goal. It is the first idea which drops into the poet's mind and it is the final idea which he last achieves in words.... I am writing of my own experiences, and my own inspiration seems to me like the faintest flash of insight into the nature of reality beside that of other poets whom I can think of.'

Intuition in philosophy:

- Jean-Jacques Rousseau, the influential French philosopher, described how on a walk from Paris to Vincennes in 1754 he

became spontaneously aware of numerous truths. These, he said, formed the basis of his philosophy.

- Bertrand Russell, twentieth-century philosopher and mathematician is quoted as saying 'In all the creative work that I have done, what has come first is a problem, a puzzle involving discomfort. Then comes a concentrated voluntary application involving great effort. After this, a period without conscious thought, and finally a solution bringing with it the complete plan of a book.'

Intuition in art:

- Max Ernst, the surrealist painter, described his method of working as, '...excluding all conscious directing of the mind (towards reason, task, or morals) and reducing to a minimum the part played by him formerly known as the author of the work....the artist's role is to gather together and then give out that which makes itself visible within him.'
- Vincent Van Gogh, the artist, wrote to his brother Theo, 'I have a lover's clear sight or a lover's blindness...I shall do another picture this very night, and I shall bring it off. I have a terrible lucidity at moments when nature is so beautiful; I am not conscious of myself any more, and the pictures come to me as in a dream...'

Intuition in science:

- Melvin Calvin, the Nobel prizewinning scientist, wrote how one day he was waiting in his car for his wife, when suddenly he was intuitively aware of the solution to the difficulties he had been experiencing in his efforts to understand aspects of the process of photosynthesis. 'It occurred just like that, quite suddenly, and suddenly also, in a matter of seconds, the path of carbon became apparent to me.' Again we see the description of an intuition as a truth recognised, rather than facts subjected to conscious evaluation and doubt.

- Friedrick Kekulé, the professor of chemistry at Ghent in 1865, had a dream or reverie which detailed how carbon and hydrogen atoms are arranged within a benzene molecule. This is one of the most important discoveries to have been made in organic chemistry. Kekulé is reported to have said, 'I turned my chair to the fire and dozed. Again the atoms were gambolling before my eyes. This time the smaller groups kept modestly in the background. My mental eye, rendered more acute by repeated visions of this kind, could now distinguish larger structures, of manifold conformation; long rows, sometimes more closely fitted together; all twining and twisting in snake like motion. But look! What was that? One of the snakes had seized hold of its own tail, and the form whirled mockingly before my eyes. As if by a flash of lightning I awoke...Let us learn to dream, gentlemen.' This vision gave Kekulé his answer; the benzene molecule is formed from a ring of carbon atoms each having hydrogen atoms attached to it.

$$
\begin{array}{c}
H \\
| \\
C \\
H-C \quad C-H \\
\| \quad \quad \| \\
H-C \quad C-H \\
C \\
| \\
H
\end{array}
$$

Benzene molecule

- Dr John Yellot, the research engineer, wrote of how he had worked very hard, without any success, on a scientific problem and was becoming obsessed with a fear of failure. 'I was riding on a crowded bus, much absorbed in...personal matters so

irrelevant to my scientific work, when suddenly the solution of the problem came to me. In a flash I visualised the drawing of the proper design of the apparatus, I immediately drew out a notebook, and, without consciousness of my surroundings, wrote down the answer. I knew it was right…'

Intuition in Mathematics:

- Henri Poincaré, the nineteenth-century French mathematician made the following four observations.

'Every day I seated myself at my worktable, stayed an hour or two, tried a great number of combinations and reached no results. One evening, contrary to my custom, I drank black coffee and could not sleep. Ideas rose in clouds; I felt them collide until pairs interlocked, so to speak, making a stable combination. By the next morning…I had only to write out the results, which took but a few hours.'

'…disgusted with my failure, I went to spend a few days at the seaside, and thought of something else. One morning, walking on the bluff, the idea came to me, with just the same characteristics of brevity, suddenness, and immediate certainty.'

'The incidents of travel made me forget my mathematical work. Having reached Cotances, we entered an omnibus to go someplace or other. At the moment when I put my foot on the step, the idea came to me, without anything in my former thoughts seeming to have paved the way for it…I did not verify the idea; I should not have had time, as, upon taking my seat in the omnibus, I went on with a conversation already commenced, but I felt a perfect certainty. On my return to Caen, for conscience' sake, I verified the result at my leisure.'

'Invention is discernment, choice. How to make this choice, I have before explained; the mathematical facts worthy of being studied are those which, by their analogy with other facts, are capable of leading us to the knowledge of a mathematical law,

just as experimental facts lead us to the knowledge of a physical law. They are those which reveal to us unsuspected kinship between other facts, long known, but wrongly believed to be strangers to one another.'

Intuition in medical research:

- Jonas Salk in 1954 developed the vaccine which has now almost eradicated poliomyelitis. Previously a widespread and greatly feared cause of paralysis, *polio* so disabled some victims that they could no longer breathe unaided. Salk is quoted as saying, 'It is always with excitement that I wake up in the morning wondering what my intuition will toss up to me, like gifts from the sea. I work with it and rely on it. It's my partner.'

Those who believe themselves to be creative and insightful seem to have the greatest success in employing their intuition. Perhaps it is a case of self-fulfilling prophesy; *as you believe, so you shall become* or merely that use and experience rewards and reinforces the behaviour. The many famous examples quoted assure us of instances of intuition which proved it to be of benefit. To be sure, intuition has proved elusive, spontaneous, and can be unpredictable, but that it occurs is, I hope, no longer in doubt. Wherever intuition comes from, we can use it, and for now, I'll settle for that.

PRACTICE

1 Do men and women experience intuition?
2 Name three examples when intuition apparently lead to a famous discovery.
3 How can we know that intuition is not conscious wishful thinking?
4 Can conscious willpower force intuition?

3 INTUITION DEVALUED

It is fashionable stupidity to regard everything one cannot explain as a fraud.

Carl Gustav Jung (1875-1961)

Intuition is a natural human faculty and like any other natural sense, it can be developed and improved. It is as important a faculty as reason, yet in recent times it has been devalued and derided. Scientists dismiss claims that intuition is our sixth sense. Intuition became unfashionable in the age of scientific, rational thought. Any topic so unpredictable, unmeasurable and unquantifiable, which does not conform to the analytic rigour of scientific testing is repudiated by science, yet ironically it is intuition which led to some of the greatest scientific discoveries, and influenced the greatest art.

If reasoning alone was enough for creativity, anyone similarly intelligent with access to the same raw data would inevitably draw the same conclusions. This just does not happen. If it did we could give a pair of rational adults identical boxes of paints, brushes and a canvas with instructions to paint the same topic and expect their artwork to be identical. They would be just as unlikely to assemble the same group of words into an identical poem. Ideas do not flow from the mere presence of facts, no matter how scientific, rational and tidy they are, and they certainly cannot be forced to appear to order. Creativity demands a little irrationality and a lot of patience.

However, times are changing and the general changes in information presentation and availability means that the old rules and

boundaries are breaking down. The advent of powerful personal tools for information gathering, such as the Internet now available at home as well as at work have helped prepare the ground. Ironically, radical changes in theoretical physics, logic, science and technology have created the conditions which make a revaluing of intuition possible.

SCIENCE AND INTUITION

Science is the metaphor of the modern age, just as formalised religion was of earlier times. What the scientific method teaches is to look for effects and results, a tendency which can lead to a neglect of causes. We record the famous successes, but choose to forget how they were arrived at. One effect of this bias is a false belief that science is a tidy methodology which moves forward in a nice, even progression. Science is certainly not seen as a place for mistakes, hunches or false starts. We rewrite history from the stance of already knowing results but give no credit to the sweat, tears and flashes of intuitive brilliance which led to the conclusions we now take as given fact. This sanitising of the role of intuition gives the intending scientist, artist or manager no clue of what is really involved in creativity and, likewise, what might enable them to succeed.

In the sixteenth century the French philosopher René Descartes decided that only pure reason could convey truth and that information gained from the senses should not be trusted. This principle became widely accepted and reason became polarised. According to Descartes, that which we cannot consciously reason we should doubt. In earlier times, when intuitions might have been interpreted as religious portents, signs from God, or the devil, the opposite extreme prevailed. There is a need today to find a middle way where we value the different resources each has to offer.

Intuition and rational thought

According to a dictionary definition, intuition is not reasonable. However, words convey more than definitions, and although it is linguistically true to call intuition unreasonable, it should not follow that we condemn it with the negative associations of that term. Reason involves conscious intent in a traceable series of events. Intuitions are single, spontaneous events. This difference should not be grounds for deciding that intuitions are therefore valueless. To be not-reasoned is not the same as to be un-reasoned. To paraphrase Lewis Carroll's *Alice in Wonderland*; I mean what I say, is not the same thing as I say what I mean.

I believe we should cherish and celebrate the fact that intuition goes beyond our reason. Reason always refers to the already known, since it employs analytic skills and thus requires data to evaluate. As valuable as the skills offered by reason are, they remain within the limits of the known. The innovators, be they geniuses or just humble employees with a talent for their job, know that intuition provides reason with fertile new ground to develop, giving an edge over competitors who restrict themselves to a reworking of the known and the commonplace. Reason is still of value, but it needs new raw materials to progress. A medical doctor needs the experience of long training and past wisdom, but confronted with a patient's symptoms it will be the synthesis of learning plus an intuitive hunch which will suggest the diagnosis and treatment.

Intuition extends knowledge beyond the limitations of reason, valuable as that skill is, to offer a tool of far greater power. It operates from the whole breadth of possibilities rather than with what we have predetermined are the relevant details. We should regard both skills as complementary rather than competing aspects of mind. To limit ourselves only to reason is to look at a colourful world through monochrome glasses.

The Limits of Reason

When we evaluate a problem using the skills of analysis and reason it is inevitable that we look through a *lens* created by our reactions to everything we have learned and experienced in our past. This past conditioning; personal, cultural and academic, shapes our impressions of how the world is, and our place in it. When we employ our reason, we cannot help but examine and analyse with reference to these acquired beliefs. Some of these accumulated beliefs are shared in common with many other people, some are shared with a particular group, and others are uniquely our own. They are not necessarily correct.

The power of thought

Our predetermined mental pathways limit the answers that our reason can supply to the problems we analyse, since we obviously cannot accurately anticipate what we have no knowledge of. It is natural to favour the facts which lend support to our pet theories, but if we are alert and pay attention to our intuition, we can learn new and perhaps more helpful solutions.

The philosopher Henri Bergson expressed this tendency to expect only what we already know in an amusing paradox which is paraphrased as follows:

- We analyse the past according to our learning and experience.
- When we do this we cannot help but add a bias which happens with any personal interpretation of an event.
- We then predict future events based on the beliefs which we have acquired as a result of what we learned in the past.
- The paradox: we now imagine the past and remember the future!

fact and certainty

Scientific statements carry a ring of authority, as though they command certainty but credibility is the property of a single mind, not a collective truth. One person's certainty is another person's doubt. We should each consider scientific claims critically and use our intuition to decide how credible we find an assertion. If any judgement is to have value we should also be free to disbelieve it. A biased jury does not dispense justice. However, with the increasing specialisations within science, we defer to those we deem to be experts, and blindly accept their truths. Science depends for its own credibility on collective value judgements, so it is hardly in a position to get high handed and say that human value judgements or intuitions are illusory. To do so undermines the status of the very system which bestows its own credibility.

History shows us that commonly held beliefs, treated as facts, can alter in the light of newer beliefs and can even be supplanted entirely over time. It was once believed by the best scientists and

the all-powerful church, and accepted as truth by most ordinary people, that the planet earth occupied the central position in the heavens. The sun, along with the other planets, were said to revolve around the earth. Copernicus discovered reasonable proofs that this was not the case, but to say so put his life in danger, since in his day it was heresy to imagine that God would have given humankind anything but the dominant position in His cosmos. Today such a belief is held by very few, regarded now as eccentrics. Even religious people generally accept that the sun occupies the central position in our solar system, which is but one of many in the universe.

Science is only the sum of our informed guesses, and objectivity only a reflection of the most popularly held theories, yet in recent times science has been raised almost to the level of a religion. One effect of scientific domination has been the undermining of other ways of understanding. Where once the arts primarily served to educate and inform by reflecting aspects of society they are often now reduced to the role of entertainment. Creativity requires an interplay between intellect and intuition. The dogma of rationalism should be challenged before we lose sight of the more balanced view.

On the personal level, supposed facts about ourselves can also be subject to change. For example, if for various reasons our life experiences did not enable us to develop a sense of self-confidence, we may believe ourselves to be of less value than others. It is possible to correct any such learned negative self-beliefs, and replace them with a more positive self-appraisal with which to enhance our interactions with others.

LANGUAGE PROBLEMS

Each era has a dominant metaphor which permeates language and thought. Definitions are drawn from language, but language is merely a collection of words as pointers to the meaning which we have collectively agreed best describes the world at any given time. A problem arises when some experiences are so personal that they

cannot be collectively communicated. Let me give an example. A blind person's personal experience of the world must differ from a sighted person's because of the non-availability of the metaphors of sight with which they can identify, make comparisons, and communicate to others. So, for example, the collectively agreed description of what we experience as yellow cannot be adequately communicated to the sightless person. Much of our language assumes a shared experience of sight to convey descriptions. The same difficulty is true of any of our other senses.

Language is essentially a public vehicle and although language reflects the dominant view of the way the world is, it is not necessarily a perfect match for what individuals experience. (Majority truth is not automatically universal truth.) Approximately one in fifty individuals are said to be colour blind and express different explanations for the experience of colour from that of the majority, but who can say for sure that the majority is right? We use the expression *mind* as though all modes of thinking were the same, yet we know from personal experience the many ways that our own mind may operate at different times. To think is not quite the same thing as to concentrate, which in turn differs from the experience of evaluating, or assuming. We use any of many modalities of thought of which intuition is experienced as just one.

There are thus particular problems for defining intuition, since intuition is a uniquely personal inner event. However, there are enough commonly described aspects to the intuitive experience to be able to claim it as a recognisable phenomenon. It has been claimed that we cannot know that of which we cannot speak. Since the connections which lead to a fully formed intuition are usually completely unknown to us, this would seem to be so.

Question your attitudes

At this point take a few minutes to consider what attitudes you have accepted unquestioningly as a person living in the scientific era. It is important to recognise the attitudes you have absorbed, so you may

freely decide if you believe them to be correct, or if they do not seem to match your instincts and observations of the world and yourself.

- Do you always have more faith in science and reason than religious or spiritual explanations?
- Do you assume that experts will always know more about your body than your own senses tell you?
- Do you believe intuition genuinely occurs?
- Are those in authority always right?
- Do you trust strong hunches, if you have them? Ask yourself these and similar questions. Ask where your attitudes came from. Were you told to accept them by parents, church, state, educators, the medical profession, the law, all those whose authority over you as a child you did not question?

WHO NEEDS INTUITION?

The question might be better put, who does not need intuition? You may or may not be the next Albert Einstein, but whatever your areas of interest, whether scientific, artistic, or others, intuition can be a useful tool for more effective and creative functioning in your personal, family, social and business life. Join the company of great inventors and creative artists who have come to trust intuition as an essential ingredient in their endeavour.

Intuition adds value to every life. Irrational yet beneficial, intuition demystified is a skill available to all. Better than guessing, as a flexible tool it aids problem solving, but it also adds the spontaneous element which identifies your endeavour as unique and precious. Once you realise that intuition is always available to you, learn how to recognise intuitive cues and how best to respond to them, you have an aid to solving your problems and enhancing your creativity. Despite these benefits, obvious to the person who has come to know the value of intuition, trying to convince those who doubt its existence can seem as daunting as trying to convince Plato's cave-dwelling prisoners of their broader reality. In both cases the reality has to be experienced first hand to be truly convincing.

Practical applications

There is value in the irrational. Learn how to free your intuition to assist you when you need to break new ground. Of course there are as many ways as there are people and problems, but the following are a few ways that intuition may be of benefit to you.

- Any creative project will come alive if it includes input from your unconscious via your intuition.
- Give an original twist to a college essay.
- A hoped for scientific or technical breakthrough may be revealed to you when the limits of your rational thought on the problem have been exhausted.
- Use your insight to suggest how best to act the role in the play you are auditioning for.
- Allow creative input from your intuition to express the emotion you want to convey via the visual mediums of paint or stone.
- Allow your intuition to add flair to your conscious planning when preparing an effective business presentation.
- Use your intuition to sense what is troubling your neighbour, friend, child or colleague, and how best to comfort or help them.
- In your international relations, add intuition to your translation and communication skills.
- If you cannot recall where you misplaced a sought for article and have searched everywhere that you can think of, give up. Let intuition provide the answer once you allow space for it to do so.
- Make your own luck. Learn to listen within to know the background situation and detect the direction which would be right for you.

PRACTICE

1 Is intuition only useful to great artists and scientists?
2 Become aware of habitual attitudes, especially concerning intuition.
3 Are all facts certain and unchanging?
4 Name two practical uses of intuition which would benefit your life.

4

INTUITION AND THE MODERN WORLD

What then is mathematics if it not a unique, rigorous, logical structure? It is a series of great intuitions carefully sifted, refined, and organised by the logic men are willing and able to apply at any time

Morris Kline, *Mathematics: The loss of certainty*

How does intuition work?

Intuition is a mental experience, so to gain some clues as to how intuition works, we will first look at some theories of how the brain functions. Later in this chapter we will also look at some theories which suggest that the brain simply acts like a receiver and interpreter, but that the mind is more than the physical brain.

The left brain/right brain model is one of several which popularly describes brain functioning. This model asserts that the two hemispheres of the brain are each responsible for different aspects of brain function.The right hemisphere is claimed to be the source of intuitive and aesthetic processing, spatial awareness, the sense of rhythm and to control the left side of the body. The left hemisphere is said to process our analytic reasoning, critical judgements, organisation of language and numbers, and to control the right side of our body. This description is the norm, in the case of a person who is dominantly right-handed and would be reversed in a predominantly left-handed person.

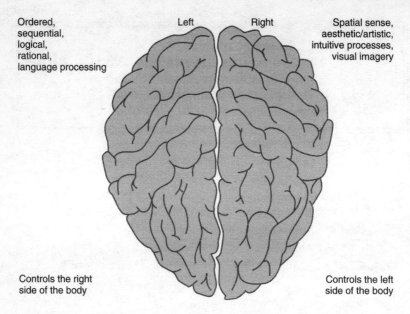

Ordered, sequential, logical, rational, language processing

Left

Right

Spatial sense, aesthetic/artistic, intuitive processes, visual imagery

Controls the right side of the body

Controls the left side of the body

The brain hemispheres and their functions (right-handed person)

The physical brain thus has the capability, to a large degree, to use either hemisphere for processing either sort of function. We know this from the cases where, following massive injury to one hemisphere, some of the functions formerly done by the damaged side have in time, been taken over by the opposite hemisphere. According to Joseph Weizenbaum's *Computer Power and human reason*, there is also considerable evidence to suggest that the right hemisphere can think independently of the left. In a person who is right-handed it is the right hemisphere of the brain which performs intuitive processing.

Weizenbaum describes the startling effects of surgery performed on severely epileptic patients. This involved severing the bridge (the corpus callosum), which links the two brain hemispheres, in an effort to halt seizures. When right-handed patients had an object, in this case a pencil, placed in their left hand, but were prevented from seeing what they held, they could still draw a picture of the object,

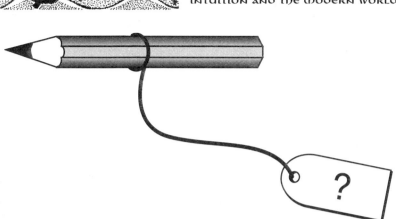

Loss of access to the left brain hemisphere

Loss of access to the right brain hemisphere

pick it out when it was presented among other, different, objects, but could not name what they held, even though they could recognise and draw it. (Naming would be controlled by the left hemisphere in a right-handed individual with surgically separated hemispheres.) The experiment was repeated on other patients who had undergone the same operation, but this time a pencil was placed in their right hand, again hidden from view. Unlike the experiment involving the

left hand, this time the patients could name the object held, but could neither draw a visual representation of the word which came to mind, nor recognise the pencil when it was presented among other objects. They had lost the concepts that would identify the word with the thing. (Spatial and artistic functions would be controlled by the right hemisphere.)

Serial processing and linear thought

Serial processing and linear thought (typically left hemisphere tasks, according to the previous model) involve the use of logical, periodic sequences: the ordering of things one at a time, from a beginning, through ordered and predictable stages, to an end. The alphabet is an example of serial/linear ordering. Of course there are no actual lines of letters in neat rows to be found within the brain, this merely describes the ordered style of processing. According to Tony Buzan, inventor of *mind mapping*, a non-linear form of making notes, when we organise information into lists and rigid sequences to learn it we make it more difficult to recall and, says Buzan, the brain functions most efficiently in a non-linear way.

Neural nets and parallel processing

Neural nets and parallel processing differ from serial processing. Scientists suggest this is a better description of how our brains function. Russian professor, Pyotr Anokhin, suggested we should be thinking of systems when considering how the brain works; that it does not function as a collection of individual parts, nor even as a complete whole. As evidence he cited that we know some brain functions have specific locations, yet others do not. Anokhin

proposed a series of interlinked and interlaced systems with multiple interactions which occurred between nodes, *as though* all were interconnected. Processing, he said, is not limited to a one-way order but occurs all at once. This neural net model of brain processing is remarkably similar to the way computer networks link up via the *Internet*, as we shall see.

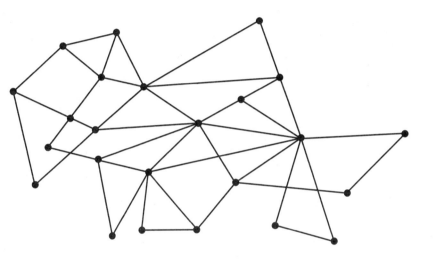

An interactively linked network of nodes

The *Internet* is not located anywhere in particular, it exists as potential linkups between sites which are connected via networks of varying size, which then connect to larger networks and so on. The connections may or may not be activated without affecting the functioning of the whole. The *Internet* is essentially a system, a potential for connections, not a fixed and permanent set. In both computer network and brain systems, if one part is damaged, other parts can take over. (Though some brain damage may be too extensive to allow this.) Perhaps when considering the brain we should therefore think of systems rather than sites.

The Internet

The *Internet* comprises individual, corporate, commercial and educational computer sites around the world. A search request using the *Internet* offers access to all of these despite the many ways information has been stored; as catalogues, individual documents, pictures, video clips and so on, and will offer the enquirer a list of all the matching references encountered. For example, an enquiry using a single keyword, *intuition*, using one of the many *search engines* available provided me with a list of over 9,000 references in English. As I write, there may be more, since entries are added all the time. Your memory will similarly offer many sample matches to an effort to recall a particular person or event, or as a response to a stimulus. Objects, dates, locations, smells, linked memories, people, letters of the alphabet, colours, all these and more may be retrieved. In some cases intuition may involve the unconscious processing and matching of information formerly encountered, but not before consciously considered. If this is the case, the parallels with an *Internet* search become more obvious.

One similarity between an *Internet* search and the functioning of our memory (and intuition), is how the search happens behind the scenes. We have no awareness of how either does so, and little information about how the process is getting on. Our only conscious awareness of memory recall, whether intuition or an *Internet* search, is by a result, whether or not the match offered accurately reflects the information we sought. We should be careful of stressing comparisons, however. Computers can seem super intelligent when all they are is fast. Similarly a genius may be completely at a loss to deal with life beyond a narrowly defined field of interest.

The *Internet* refers more accurately to a potential link between sites, or more imaginatively, the virtual space between things rather than the things themselves. Intuition seems to be a process which can sift the infinite potentiality of all known things, even delving into the spaces in between a definite this or a that, sifting all the maybes as well, until it forms into a link which answers the focused transmission of a question.

Networks

A brief explanation of the history and development of the *Internet* might be helpful if you are not yet actively involved in its use. I hope that by taking a closer look at the structure of the *Internet*, comparisons with the way we access our intuition will be apparent.

In the 1960s the government of the United States of America decided that their defence plans were vulnerable if key information sites came under attack (primarily those occupied with military or research work, including the large universities doing military funded research). At each site the information systems were based upon a single powerful central computer connected to satellite terminals which could not communicate with each other, only with the parent central computer. It was decided that the risk to defence could be limited by creating a network linking the major computer installations in such a way that even if any individual site were to be destroyed, the ability of the remainder to communicate would not be compromised.

The original network linked up just three computer sites in California and one in Utah, but soon other university sites clamoured to be allowed to join this network for the ease of communications it offered in all areas of research. This ever growing network was fast becoming unmanageable, so it was decided to separate the military aspects into a smaller network, known as MILNET leaving the remainder as the more manageable ARPANET. In time the ARPANET was superseded by NSFNET (National Science Foundation network) which in turn was replaced by the commercial networks of today forming immeasurably more links than was envisaged by the original educational and military sites. It was decided to keep a standard means of communication so that each of these networks could still speak to each other although now separated, and a protocol was the technical means devised to achieve this. As a result of this decision each site is an equal part of a dynamic system and can communicate with any other site also connected to the network. This removed the need for communications command centres.

The development of an *Internet* protocol marked the birth of the true *Internet* in 1982. Protocols have been the basis of the continued growth and connectability of the *Internet*, which in reality consists of millions of individual sites, linked to thousands of regional networks, all routed via the backbone network of supercomputers to which the smaller networks link up. In the beginning the network involved only mainframe computers (very large computers) operating mainly with the UNIX computer language which required specialist training to use, (less user friendly than modern personal computers). It was barely conceivable that from this original situation, hundreds of thousands of personal computers would be connected within a few years, via the *Internet*, as they are today. Access to the *Internet* is gained by means of a *service provider*, a company which maintains access to these frequently used sites via whichever route is most accessible at a given time. This speeds up access for users, but the *Internet*, and world wide collection of web sites upon it, consists of far more potential sites than are regularly kept in contact by these companies.

The backbone of supercomputers to which the regional networks are connected, are linked through very fast, high capacity lines to cope with the volumes of data they convey. Today it is the same dynamic routing originally designed to protect military secrets, which operates throughout the *Internet* so that theoretically, any attack or mishap occurring to one site can not disable the whole. Following damage or disruption, information flows through other, undamaged routes, like water finding a path around an obstacle. To put this more graphically imagine the difference between a car and a train which regularly travel from Paris to London. If the train track is blocked or damaged the journey cannot be made. However, a car encountering a blocked or damaged road would still get to London by using a different route, passing through different towns as it did so.

The dynamic method used by the *Internet* to assure delivery of its messages was tested in 1991 when the US government was unable to disable the Iraqi command network. It was found that the Iraqi military were using the standard network routing and recovery technology, which was so infinitely adjustable it could not be

breached. If all the host sites on the *Internet* were to close there would still be ways to network by using *bulletin boards, newsgroups* and *e-mail*. An individual can cross into uncharted territory, and make contact with anyone anywhere who is linked to the network, if they have the know-how. The pathways chosen to do this may be quite unique and to a degree, hunches and intuition play a part. Nonetheless, the *Internet* can only connect what is there.

Packet switching

The way this rerouting is achieved in the transmission of data from one place to another on the *Internet*, is by means of technology called *packet switching*. Instead of sending the transmission as a single document from one site to another via a fixed route, which would be open to interception or destruction, the information is broken up into small packets, each communication being preceded with facts about its destination and transmission addresses, plus details of which other packets it connects with when it arrives.

Each packet may also carry an error checking code. Parity is one example; the sum of the binary code in the packet should match the parity label which accompanies it to verify its integrity as it passes the bridges or routers which connect separate networks. Each connection is able to read the addressing data on each packet and send it on, via whichever route is open. This does away with the need for a central, controlling computer which would be vulnerable to interference. If the data comprising a packet is found to have been compromised when checked at any of these points, the bridge or router requests that the packet be sent again and depending on the state of the dynamic system, it may go by quite different router the next time. The packets can contain all manner of digitally stored information such as text, colour graphics, computer programs, videos, and sound or voice files. They can be sent via a portable computer and mobile telephone as easily as from an office or home. Locating the source to interrupt transmission is thus nearly impossible.

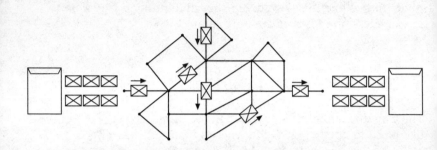

Packet routing with integrity checking

It is for technical rather than political reasons, that the various packets which comprise your message will be sent via different routes due to the dynamic nature of the system. The bridge used for the first packet may be different from the one used when the next packet departs but all the packets are finally reunited for verification that they accurately delivered the original message, when they reach the intended destination. Thus if a branch of the network is cut, or a part of the message is intercepted, the complete message will fail the verification checks and the packets will be automatically resent and rerouted through undamaged channels. This all happens at blindingly fast speeds so that a large chunk of data can be sent across the world in seconds, its packets being verified and passed on, or rejected and resubmitted as necessary.

INTUITION AND MEMORY

Information, we know, is as much shaped by the knowledge of the person who receives it as by the means which transmitted it, be that organic, digital or mechanical. Emotion plays no small part in the shaping of an individual's knowledge but plays no part in a computer's. The human mind as far as we know does not make a search through the brain in a linear way. On the contrary our minds seem to retrieve information by simultaneously scanning the available source material in a more holistic way.

For the time being, at least, computers and human beings do not process information in the same way. However, there is an *apparent* similarity between a human and a computer when retrieving information from memory, or from a search via the *Internet*. In both cases, there is a search for any possible items which match the criteria we have defined. We act as if a computer were intelligent when we assume it can complete the tasks we set it, but in reality a computer deals with unimaginable complexity at incredibly fast speeds, but without what we would consider to be intelligence or true intuition. The position may change in the future. The fact that the information processing occurs out of sight and we are only aware of computer *thinking* time followed by a result, can mislead us into imagining intelligence, because efforts to retrieve information from our memory appears to follow along similar lines. Arguments rage as to whether computers could ever be deemed intelligent but that they can behave now as though they were, seems beyond much dispute.

No theory of human memory or intuition will exactly fit the reality, since like all theories and models, it only symbolises a reality which remains beyond the symbols used to represent it. The map can never be the territory and should not be mistaken for it. As far as we know at present, the human mind does not use an information retrieval system anything like the linear format of a book or catalogue ordered from A to Z, though its actual workings remain the subject of debate. However, it can seem as though the methods of human memory retrieval are somewhat like those used in modern technological communications.

The *Internet* offers an opportunity to search for specific information by means of large computers, made accessible to individual use, via the multiple networks which comprise the *Internet*. These so called *search engines* use programs and matching protocols designed to find the information you require with such blinding speed that they give every appearance of behaving in the same way as our memory.

It is tempting to compare observable behaviour and assume similar processes. Facts are not of themselves knowledge. It is not until facts get classified and cross referenced to other already known information that they add to knowledge. This process requires that there be rules for selection or exclusion set up by an intelligence above and beyond the facts themselves. In the case of humans, this would be a reasoning mind, in the case of a computer, a software program which is capable of operating apart from its creator, but which depends upon the criteria a human has set for it, which it can only obey. This distinction is becoming fuzzier, however.

Jeff Instone's *Hypertopography* offers us programs with the potential of multiple multidimensional connections which vary according to user interactions with the program. The program responds dynamically to the user's progress through the information base. This is a fancy description for what happens in the interactive games and reference works which are now so popular on home computers. Such computer *behaviour* gets pretty close to what we see when observing human information retrieval.

Computer scientists are working towards the day when machines can emulate intuition. Some progress has been made. It is now possible for a computer to adapt to personal handwriting given some examples from which to learn the style. Thus your intended meaning can be accurately typed from what may have been a scribbled note on an electronic pad. Rather than having an inbuilt example of every possible word that you may write, against which the computer finds a match, the computer makes guesses and performs pattern matching similar to how you or I do when attempting to make sense of someone else's handwriting. Neural query software programs use *neural networks* and *fuzzy logic* to offer answers to inexact questions. They suggest the most suitable next word, from an understanding of the context of what has gone before, and a concept dictionary. It is

also possible for programs to respond to spoken instructions rather than written or typed input. The redundancy of typists implied by such advances is in part counterbalanced by the possibility of expanding the horizons of the physically handicapped.

Memory appears to operate by parallel processing, breaking up into many search directions rather like the *packet switching* of the *Internet*, to cohere only when the answer is complete. As with the *packet switching* analogy, this may involve some failed connections at first. We all know how it is to want to recall the name of a particular person or place only to have the mind suggest the nearest match it can come up with, that the name begins with a certain letter of the alphabet or that we associate it with a particular person or place.

When we recall sought for items from our memory, by a process of matching from all the records of events of which we have ever been aware, we connect those possibilities which seem to fit the bill, and reject those that do not. This process occurs without our awareness until a potential match is offered for our conscious evaluation. If a mismatch is retrieved from memory we resubmit the enquiry, unless we have no further interest in the correct answer. Our inner *search engines*, to use an *Internet* term, continue the process of looking until we are aware of the correct match or we give up the attempt, in the case of the human mind, by having our attention distracted by ongoing events around us. We may simply have lost interest, or tired of the effort. (It is, however, more often than not when we stop thinking that the answer enters consciousness.)

Some would say that intuition is merely the retrieval of facts that we have been exposed to but have forgotten. Our minds select what is currently relevant and make dormant the material not necessary for our present needs. In normal waking states we are not able to recall all the data we have ever experienced since birth, yet some say it is there, given the means of retrieval. If it is so it would help to explain the workings of intuition.

If our minds did not filter out the irrelevant we would be swamped by all the information our senses detect, quite apart from the items we normally think of as residing in memory. These are some of the justifications for a potential total recall.

- Under hypnosis we seem to recall more than our conscious mind is capable of.
- According to the practitioners and clients of *rebirth* techniques, even the moment of our birth can be made conscious again.
- It is commonplace for individuals to experience dreams in which places and people from the long forgotten past are present with striking clarity, yet they had been totally erased from conscious recall.
- It said by some who have been near to death that we recall all that has gone before, even persons long forgotten.
- Memories from the distant past can be reactivated by some medication, which suggests we store more than we know.
- Some people claim that past lives can be recalled under regressive hypnosis.

There is obviously much to the mind that remains to be explained, but unless we favour a mystical explanation for intuition, a sort of Platonic realm of perfection and a cosmic warehouse of all possibilities from which we can occasionally withdraw the items we need, the idea that intuition involves the resifting of items we have previously been exposed to is an attractive, and rational explanation.

Complex change

Developments made by specialists in the fields of modern mathematics, science and technology gradually reach mass awareness. Once these new concepts become commonly known, the work of individual artists and inventors becomes affected, whether they are conscious or unconscious of the influence. We then get many interpretations of the same original material and the previous, rigid subject boundaries become weakened. Changes which began in specialist areas start to have ever more complex effects.

It was the philosopher Aristotle who classified all forms of being into an inventory. He set out lists of categories having predetermined what properties must be present to be included in a category. According to

such precise logic, all is clear cut, but life has other ideas. There is a problem with such rigid categorisation. Whilst the systems devised by human intellect, such as number, measurement and time, may behave in a predictable fashion, very little in nature is as tidy. For instance, when is the moment when becoming old happens? Would that be universally true for all people? Is a tall building constructed in New York in 1900 still a tall building in 1997? How long is a long wait?

There has been a gradual weakening of the former stranglehold of dualistic ways of thinking, the tendency to assume that there must be an either/or, yes/no, black/white, on/off, answer. The old rigid definitions are gradually being replaced by more complex categories, across the whole of culture. In art we see more liberal interpretations of the relationships of objects and space, and a move towards abstraction. In technology systems are now designed using the concepts of *fuzzy logic*, states in between definite yes or no, on or off positions, varying according to interactive need. In society, gender distinctions are less certain.

How did this change happen? First the work of eminent physicists and logicians made scientists aware of new principles which suggested that there is an underlying uncertainty and chaos operating in the world which for centuries science had worked so hard to make predictable. Word about uncertainty gradually leaked out to the wider world, and then with the popularisation of science through books and mass media, the influence of these ideas spread. As a result we increasingly allow for maybes, sometimes and shades of grey. The development of *fuzzy logic* may seem such obvious commonsense now that it should not need stating, but western logic for centuries adopted the principle of duality. A thing was either the case or not. *Fuzzy logic* is now used in science and computer technology to rethink new approaches to old problems. It is even possible that you enjoy some of the results of a break from dualistic logic in your own home. *Fuzzy logic* has been incorporated into many household systems such as washing machines and central heating systems.

Even once highly controlled and rigidly determined business institutions have made tentative moves toward a re-evaluation of formerly rigid roles. In 1997 a respected British law firm recruited a

poet-in-residence to encourage a freer use of the language than that normally used when dealing with clients. Other organisations have expressed a desire to do likewise. Brainstorming, a known technique for freeing creativity in advertising, has become accepted practice in forward thinking boardrooms. Some companies which were once rigidly hierarchical have set up systems to encourage and enable staff at all levels to input ideas, without fear or favour, and have been surprised to find a wealth of hidden talent.

Finally I want to mention some theories which seem to suggest that our minds are more than merely physical brains and which, if true, offer other possibilities for an understanding of how intuition may function.

The collective unconscious

Science has found no mechanism or part of the human organism which is capable of making intuitive connections beyond the realm of the individual, such as is claimed in some esoteric beliefs, though this does not prove it to be impossible. Such a realm of potential information which can respond to individual need, remains untraceable, yet creates interactions which will take quite some explaining. The psychologist Carl Jung expressed his belief in a collective unconscious, a pool of future potential and past experience, which may interact in just this mysterious way. Through interaction with collective consciousness we touch the universal symbols of humanity which shape the myths and legends of all cultures. In humans, the instances of intuition, ESP and synchronicity may serve to suggest Jung was correct. Since individual and collective unconsciousness would by definition be beyond conscious awareness, we could only infer their existence by observed phenomena and results.

Morphic resonance

We see something like an intuitive group mind at work in a beehive or anthill, in shoals of fish and migrating flocks of birds. Rupert Sheldrake, a British biologist, proposes a sort of energy field which operates by what he calls morphic resonance. According to his theory of formative causation, when one member of a species acquires a new skill the resonance affects all other members, like the ripples of a pebble dropped into a pond.

It seems that once a single rat was taught a new skill, such as the way to get through a maze, other rats learned the same skill much faster than the original rat. The conclusion drawn was that though unrelated, the other rats had somehow acquired a predisposition to perform the same skill. Sheldrake proposes that they inherit this predisposition through the effect of morphic resonance, which is unconnected to genetics.

Another frequently quoted example is known as the *Hundredth monkey*. A single female monkey on a Japanese island was observed to solve the problem of how to effectively remove sand from sweet potatoes found on the beach, by washing them in the sea before eating them. At first she, alone, knew how to get the sand off the potatoes but others soon imitated her. So far this may seem unremarkable, but what was noted next lends support to Sheldrake's theory. Once a critical number of monkeys had learned how to clean their potatoes, suddenly it seemed they all knew how, rather than learning one from another. More remarkable still, so did monkeys on other islands, which had no contact with the original group. The evidence for these claims is disputed, of course, but if a resonance could be proved, it might also help to explain precognitive intuitions, the times when you know something before you realistically could have done.

Sheldrake's more recent work involves investigating the morphic resonance which he says links pets with their owners. He has set up experimental conditions to record animal behaviour at the moment when the owner decides to leave work to return home. With video

cameras recording the human and animal behaviour throughout the day, it could be seen that the person had only to think of leaving to dramatically affect the actions of the pet at home. The pets were filmed all day, resting, eating and moving around the home, but at the moment of the owner deciding to go home the pet would become instantly animated, running to the door or window in anticipation, even when apparently sleeping moments before.

Sheldrake had his human subjects break with their normal routines but still the pets sensed the moment when their owner was about to return. Sheldrake even asked another person to make the decision when to tell the worker to go home without telling him or the pet owner when that might be beforehand. He repeated these tests over several days, without setting any pattern that the animal might adapt to, yet the pet always sensed the moment of the decision to return home. Replaying the separate films with a split screen and the elapse times visible, showed that only a few seconds delay occurred between the thought, and the pet's response, regardless of routine or surprise.

If energy fields such as morphic resonance are all around us, like radio waves, it could be that when we experience strong emotions, as when in earnest prayer, deep grief, or spiritual longing, we create a focus or link which elicits a response from this energy field. This might also be a fruitful area for studying how intuition works, which could support the claims that intuition operates beyond the limitations implied by the brain and memory analogies.

PRACTICE

1 Which side of your brain controls intuitive processing according to left-brain, right-brain theory?
2 In a right-handed person which hemisphere of the brain is said to control reason?
3 What is *packet switching*?
4 What is different about *fuzzy logic*?

5

kNOW YOUR OWN INTUITION

*When I am, as it were, completely myself, entirely alone, and of
good cheer – say, travelling in a carriage, or walking after a good
meal, or during the night when I cannot sleep; it is on such
occasions that my ideas flow best and most abundantly....
Whence and how they come, I know not; nor can I force them.*

Wolfgang Amadeus Mozart (1756–91)

RECOGNISING INTUITION

We are so used to relying upon our powers of reason that to
expect any other aspect of our mental faculty to give us useful
information seems contradictory. The non-rational has become
equated with the irrational. The habit of classifying in advance what
form information should take before we will listen to it creates
problems. Such a bias makes it difficult to recognise and benefit
from intuition as a useful resource.

Intuition generally seems to occur when we are not thinking about
the subject it concerns. It is as if intuition must wait for our rational
mind to quit its domination of our thought patterns. There is
perhaps only a few moments when there is an opportunity to get the
message through, before the barrier of our habitual way of thinking
returns. This fleeting and quixotic method of delivery goes against
all the instincts of the person who relies totally on traceable facts
and hard reason. The annoying thing, however, is that intuition

works. It would be so much more convenient to the confirmed rationalist to be able to dismiss the works inspired by intuitive input as irrational nonsense, but then we would also have to dismiss the most famous works of Einstein, Mozart and Newton, to name but three. Ask anyone who has learned to trust and utilise their intuition and you will discover that they are not irrational beings, merely average people who use their minds in a more holistic way, some of whom seem to be gifted innovators with a knack for spotting trends or making discoveries from material others had overlooked.

The intuitive process is not limited by our rationally known pathways. It is only when these are relaxed, as when our attention is at rest, or directed elsewhere, that the intuitive answer can present itself to our consciousness. Perhaps we create barriers to infinite possibility by our belief in limitations which, when momentarily dropped, allow other realities. Let intuition be a tool. We should learn to trust non-rational perceptions if we want to increase receptivity to intuition. To do so we must learn to listen and observe. We need to become familiar with our feelings and to observe them with detachment and without censureship.

There used to be a well-paid and rather unusual job in farming, that of chicken sexing. Intuitive people were employed to separate the male and female chicks, because few males are wanted. This was done before the chicks showed any outward sexual characteristics, yet a good chicken sexer worked at speed as they came along a conveyor belt. This improbable skill was tested by allowing the growth of selected chicks to an age when their sexual characteristics were plain. The sexers were found to have been accurate to a degree which far outstripped statistical probability. When asked how they did it, they answered that did not know how, they simply knew.

We know that intuition is often accompanied by an intensity of feeling, a sense of excitement or anxiety, coupled with a feeling of certainty. To increase your receptivity to intuition it is therefore helpful if you become more familiar with your feelings, and learn to experience them without censure. If your personality favours rationality above other mental faculties, this aspect of perception may need your particular attention. In some cases the desire to act

upon an inexplicable feeling may be an expression of intuition. The following tale serves to illustrate the importance of acknowledging such a clear urge.

The English actor, Sir Alec Guinness tells a story of his only meeting with the young American actor, James Dean. It seems that Dean greatly admired the older actor's work, and asked that he join his table in an otherwise full restaurant. Alec Guinness gladly accepted. In a moment of enthusiasm at this unexpected meeting, James Dean asked if he could show him something first. In the parking lot of the restaurant Dean proudly revealed his new silver sports car, a Porsche 550 Spyder. What happened next surprised Guinness, but however odd it seemed, he felt compelled to say what he felt so strongly. He told Dean that he must never drive that car and that it was now ten o'clock on Friday 23 September 1955 and that if Dean did drive it, he would be found dead in it by the this time next week. Probably not knowing what to say to such a pronouncement, Dean shrugged off the remark and they entered the restaurant without more ado. Sadly the prediction came true when James Dean was killed at the wheel of his new car on his way to a race meeting the following Friday. Sir Alec says he has never had such an experience before or since, but he knew he must speak out at the risk of seeming foolish, because he felt it so strongly, though he was meeting this young man for the first time.

In modern physics, Werner Heisenberg demonstrated that at the subatomic level it is impossible to make measurements of which we are certain. The act of taking one measurement causes a change in the other elements yet to be measured. This discovery became known as the *Uncertainty Principle*. What has this to do with intuition? If we assume that the only source of truth is our capacity to reason, we have already limited the answers we can receive, and we will frame our questions in ways which reason alone can answer. It would be unlikely as well as illogical for us to do otherwise. If the answer to a problem lies in grasping the interaction of various components as a whole, and all we look for is a single cause, we will have blinkered ourselves to realising the truth. If we insist on evaluating everything by the rules of reason we have no way to

measure the unreasoned. As the psychologist Abraham Maslow said, 'If your only tool is a hammer, you begin to see everything in terms of nails.'

Imagine if we knew for a fact that all cats have four legs and a tail. Is a Manx cat, which has no tail, therefore not a cat? This is the sort of problem rigid categories and rules of measurement do not allow for. When we rigidly insist on using only our familiar mental pathways, we predetermine the nature an answer must take. This erects a barrier to the help our intuition can give us.

We have seen how our preconceptions can lead us to misinterpret an intuitive message. Perhaps you find the intuitional suggestion so unusual that you doubt it, and so continue to apply familiar explanations rather than risk the new ones offered. Maybe you just do not want to believe the intuitive message because it contradicts what you believe to be the case. Such missed intuitions will only be shown to have been true with the wisdom of hindsight unfortunately, but if as a result we learn to respect such valuable information in the future, they will not have been completely wasted.

Synchronicity

The term synchronicity was coined by the Swiss psychologist Carl Jung who noted, in certain patients, occasional instances of a connection between psychic states and objective events which had no apparent cause. At times the intensity of a patient's unexpressed inner world seemed to elicit a physical, tangible response from the outer world, in the form of a material coincidence. This is more than those chance coincidences which have no connecting meaning, such as when you receive a letter from someone whom you had thought of for the first time in years only the day before. It is meaning which determines synchronicity as Jung intended the term.

The most famous of his quoted examples involves a patient who had a rigid belief in logical and rational thinking, and who was unable to understand a dream in which she had been given a golden scarab beetle. At the moment of relating this dream to Jung there came the

sound of a gentle tapping at the closed window behind him. He turned to see an insect battering itself against the glass in an apparent attempt to enter. On opening the window Jung caught what he recognised to be the nearest locally occurring equivalent to the scarab beetle of the dream. The patient had no knowledge until told by Jung that the golden scarab symbolised rebirth in Egyptian mythology, yet the aptness of the dream image and the physical manifestation served its purpose nonetheless. The nudge to the patient's consciousness resulted in her understanding the meaning of her dream and being able to accept that she was ready to begin a new way of interpreting the world.

This case is interesting as an indication of a natural interactive link between individuals and their environment, since if this had been a supernatural experience, one might have expected the more fantastic appearance of an actual scarab beetle. In *Becoming Prosperous – a beginner's guide* (1997), another book in this series, I describe another instance of synchronicity known to me personally. *A dreamer witnessed a funeral procession in which a coffin was being carried by hooded figures, like monks or nuns. Following behind, the dreamer entered a church and noticed with particular attention, a 50 pence coin on the floor in the doorway. Stepping over this, the dreamer took a seat in the church. The funeral procession disappeared as it crossed the threshold. Looking around, the dreamer recalled all the other persons present from childhood, faces now seen vividly which could no longer be called to mind in the waking state. Surprised to see and remember these people, the dreamer now noted a table, on which were examples of a hobby successfully enjoyed during schooldays. Sensing that the teacher was about to come in and praise the dreamer's work, which was on top of the pile, the dreamer re-experienced feelings of pleasure, pride and self-denying embarrassment as was the case in childhood when singled out for praise. The dream ended.*

The meaning of the dream was half suspected by the dreamer, but was not acted upon. Synchronicity provided the nudge which finally made the meaning clear. Some while after having the dream a 50 pence coin literally dropped out of the sky at the dreamer's feet. This was so startling that it immediately brought the dream back to mind and emphasised the deep importance of its message. Now the dreamer recognised and accepted the importance of the dream talent.

Rationally one may say a bird such as a magpie or jackdaw dropped the coin, as was probably the case, but the nudge to understanding the dream's meaning was as effective as had been the beetle in Jung's example. This dreamer was to become 50 years of age in the following year. This birthday was perceived as a threshold moment, and a time for evaluating life so far. The dream indicated that it was time for old habits to die, as depicted symbolically by the pun of religious robes, or habits worn by the coffin's pallbearers. The feelings in the church mirrored those the dreamer would experience at school when praised by a teacher for work done. Afraid that praise would cause alienation from friends, the child had repressed and belittled the hobby, and continued to as an adult. The secret desire to work in this way remained in the unconscious. This dream was clearly saying that the time had come to break the habit of self-denigration, and cross the threshold to reclaim that forgotten skill. The synchronous event shocked the meaning into consciousness.

YOUR INTUITION

Take a moment or two to think about what intuition means to you. Perhaps you find it difficult to believe that you have any intuition. The following are just some suggestions of how you may be experiencing it already, but so naturally that you took it for granted. The more self-aware you become the more likely you are to free yourself from the rigid thinking which blocks intuition.

- Do you ever just know a thing without knowing how you know?
- Have you ever known your way around a place that you had no prior knowledge of, and had not previously visited?
- Were you ever about to undertake a task, when out of the blue, you suddenly felt completely certain about the outcome? (Not mock certainty as when trying to convince yourself, by the willed act of positive thinking. More a blind sense of absolute certainty, when only moments before you had no idea either way.)
- Have you ever seen in your mind's eye, the flash of a scene other than the one you have before you?

- Do you sometimes just know that someone will prove to be a problem, or a benefit to you? (Again, this has the quality of certainty, not of conscious prejudice, nor wishful thinking.)
- Have you ever sensed you were being watched before you knew whether you were, much less by whom?
- Have you ever pondered the solution to a problem, using all your rational powers of analysis and then given up, only to have the correct answer come to you when you are no longer consciously thinking about the problem at all?
- Did you ever ignore a negative hunch about a person or situation only to realise later the justification for it?

TRUST AND WISE CAUTION

When I suggest that intuition can be recognised as the gift of truth I do not mean to imply that there is no need to check its reliability, and practicability. It would be a reckless soul who chose to live entirely at the bidding of intuitive prompting before learning by long experience how to discriminate between genuine intuition, and self-deception. No scientist worthy of the name would proceed blindly, purely on the strength of an intuition, and neither should we. We must learn discrimination. When a decision must be made, take a few minutes away from distractions, to feel for your intuitive reaction. If you feel a clear response, you can make a decision, whether for or against, but if you are unsure, you then have the chance to play for time, or decline, until you have a clear sense of direction.

Arthur Koestler in his book, *The Act of Creation*, (1964) describes a survey of scientists concerning their use of intuition. Of those asked, 83 per cent claimed that intuition played a part in their work. However these scientists went on to say that the intuitions were found to have varying degrees of accuracy from 90 per cent claimed by some, to only 10 per cent by others. Only 7 per cent of these scientists claimed their intuition had proved to be 100 per cent accurate on every occasion. The diversity of these results might seem disheartening until one considers that if a similar survey were

done, using the same number of cases, but this time where the only means of tackling scientific problems had been rational analysis, the results may have been no less varied. The Koestler survey does not make such comparisons however. In any case, the private nature of an intuitive experience creates problems for authenticating results of the sort of Koestler's survey.

Discrimination

It takes time and experience to hone your intuition, just as it did the other aspects of your mind. It is thus sensible to use the best of your rationality as well as your intuition. Let each mental skill enhance the capacity of the other in harmonious wisdom. Practise reality testing by checking out intuitive suggestions before enacting them. I suspect that if an intuition proves to be only partly right; for example if the idea was right, but the timing wrong; the error probably lies with our understanding and interpretation, not with the intuitive information itself. Fortunately it is perfectly possible to utilise reason and intuition to the maximum of which you are capable, without diminishing the quantity available of either. After all, intuition and reason are both merely concepts and definitions; signs to describe dynamic processes which should not be taken as literal descriptions of tangible objects.

PRACTICE

1 What is the determining characteristic, according to Carl Jung, of a synchronistic event?
2 How do habitual ways of thinking prove a barrier to intuition?
3 Give an example of an intuition in your personal experience.
4 What do discrimination and reality testing have to do with intuitions?

6 FREE YOUR INTUITION

Work brings inspiration, if inspiration is not discernable at the beginning.

Igor Stravinsky (1882–1971), *Chronicles of my life*, 1935

First let us remind ourselves of the general principles, before we look at some useful techniques you may use to enhance and encourage intuition. Intuition can be coaxed, but never commanded. We must stop trying to make something happen if we want to encourage intuition. Intuition requires a pre-rational, or non-rational state of mind, so there is no profit in using conscious deliberation and determination, however stern or sincere. We need to remove the everyday mental blocks which are keeping intuitions at bay. It is a state of awareness that is needed, not of reason. However, rational thought can be used to determine the focus of our interest to which intuitions may or may not add insight. The rational mind lights the beacon, following which we must trust and hope.

Rational effort

When you have a specific area of concern it helps to have prepared the ground first by exercising as much conscious effort upon the problem as you can. This rational effort will form the framework, or vessel, for intuitions. Artists have described how they must hold the tension between a passive state, receptive to intuition, but at the same time use their practical, conscious skills and talent as the

medium through which intuitions may appear. This double act can be like walking a tightrope.

Without the initial focus, we would be unaware of intuitions even if we were surrounded by them. By making a rational mental effort to solve the problem we focus, and become ready to notice the response. How would we recognise an answer if we have not yet formulated the question? So, think, analyse and try to solve the problem rationally; try out any creative avenues you know of to solve the task, using whatever medium is suitable. Talk to others, make notes, experiment, attempt trial solutions. To recap:

- Define the issue using your rational faculties to the full.
- Gather as much relevant information as you can from all the sources you can think of, *online* facilities, public reference libraries, art galleries, museums, company records, manufacturers of materials, whatever seems useful.
- Concentrate on the topic. Bring all your powers of reason to bear on it. Think about the problem at every opportunity and analyse it to the best of your ability.
- Create experimental models, debate, employ paint and canvas, pen and paper, wood and wool, books, computer programs, whatever is available and seems relevant.

Allow plenty of time for reason. You may find an adequate solution this way which is fine. On this occasion you do not need to draw on your intuition. If, however, you try as hard as you know how but still cannot resolve the difficulty, acknowledge the fact and give your intuition a try.

Clear the decks

Organise your time as far as is practicable to allow for free fermentation of ideas. This may mean finding a peaceful corner or could mean immersing yourself in everyday pursuits which take little or no thought. Quiet reflection is as valuable as analytic thinking. It has been reported that activities such as reading, watching a film or

television, listening to music, meditating, gardening, taking a bus or car ride, walking, swimming, or soaking in the bath have lead to intuitional breakthroughs. To recap:

- Be prepared to receive the solution, but do not think about it.
- Even when relaxing, always have pen and paper or recording device to hand.
- Stay open to possibilities, suspend disbelief and allow yourself to be surprised by potential solutions.
- Assume your problem can be solved and that you have the necessary creativity and expertise.

Do not make the desire for a response the focus for anxiety, or feel that something must be received today. A tense mind will just be another variant of your everyday thought patterns and will act as a closed door to intuitions.

Surrender

Here is a paradox. Having tried so hard to solve the dilemma with your reason you should now give up. You cannot control unconscious processes so it is pointless to try to be intuitive. If you could consciously will them, they wouldn't be unconscious processes. You can control the frame, or vessel but not what will fill it. You have set your goals and worked as best you can to solve the problem, now you must allow your mind freedom without interference, and the best way to do so is to do something of a totally different nature. Case histories have shown that intuition functions best when the rational mind is at rest, in free fall, or at least focused on another issue. It is therefore helpful to reproduce these conditions in order to tap into this source of wisdom. Intuition slips past a mind which is barely ticking over much more easily than one tied up with conscious effort, so choose an activity which does not require concentrated effort.

Have patience. You need to suspend your reliance on rational and analytic thought and must be willing to accept the possibility of learning from intuition. If you are impatient, you are still trying to be

controlling, which is an act of the conscious mind. Also be aware of resistance. Perhaps you were taught to value reason so strongly that you nurture a subtle wish to prove intuition does *not* work. This takes the form of a deep-seated doubt which will undermine the process. Reread the famous examples of intuition and trust that it is unlikely that *all* were mistaken. If you have deep-seated doubt or negativity toward the success of the process, do not be surprised if your mind confirms your belief. The will is a powerful instrument which obeys your deeper desires, not your outward pretence.

It helps if what you choose to do is not another task involving a lot of rational thinking, because that may prevent intuitions from getting through to your attention. Allow your thoughts to wander, observe images and ideas but do not direct them. What good are intuitions if we so saturate our mind with thinking and speaking that we cannot hear them? Too often we give scant attention to another person's speech because we are more concerned with what we want to say next. If you have a radio tuned to one station you cannot receive the transmissions from another.

The story of the man who regarded himself as a serious seeker after truth serves to make the point. After years of searching for a famous spiritual teacher, at last he found his whereabouts. The teacher invited the young man to enter his house and asked if he would like a cup of tea, which he gratefully accepted. As he poured the tea the teacher asked the young man why he had come. The seeker proceeded to tell the teacher of all the hardships which had prompted his quest, of how he had heard tell of this wonderful teacher, and of the trials and tribulations he had experienced before finding him. The teacher meanwhile continued to pour the young man's cup of tea which reached the rim of the cup, spilled over onto the table and even to the floor but still the teacher poured. The young man did not wish to seem disrespectful, but felt he must alert the teacher to this misjudgment, and urgently did so. The teacher paused and replied, 'You are like this cup, my son. When you decide you are ready to learn, come to me empty, until then I bid you farewell.' Upon which he bowed and left the room. The seeker frantically searched the building and courtyard but the teacher had vanished leaving him to ponder for many more years how his own

foolishness had wasted this opportunity. If we give little or no attention to the teaching from our inner wisdom we also miss guidance there for the taking. To recap:

- Once you have become aware of the problem and have done your rational best, walk away, literally or mentally. Let it be. To misquote an old saying; If at first you don't succeed, give up.
- Recognise it is necessary to rest when you have exhausted all known avenues.
- Do something completely different, preferably something which relaxes you. Be playful. If you have a hobby involving repetitive actions, so much the better.
- Learn to listen. Meditate or pray if you can, and listen to your inner prompting. Watch your emotional reactions in your daily activities and be open to chance encounters.
- Be aware of any negative programming which is causing you to resist intuitive guidance. You cannot deceive your own mind.
- Intuition does not conflict with any religious belief. Indeed, revelation has been an element in the highest religious life of many faiths. Intuition is an aspect of your humanity, whether or not you consider that to be God given. You need not resist it.
- If you are habitually tense, massage, aromatherapy, reflexology, yoga or Tai Ch'i exercises may help relieve stress and increase your receptivity.
- Have faith that the answer will come to you, although you may have to wait a while. Remember, the process is effortless. Effort involves the will and conscious thought, which blocks intuition.
- Intuition will not flow where it is not valued. Be aware of your belief system, and allow for the possibility of learning something new, at whatever age.
- Trust that you have sown the seeds and give them a chance to germinate.
- If you feel stuck, use your imagination. The following is an example you may like to try:

You see a house. You enter and wander around, examining the rooms and the objects in them. You see a door to the basement and decide to explore there. In the floor of the basement is a trapdoor. You lift the trapdoor and climb down the steep steps before you. You reach tunnels

63

which run deep, deep beneath the house. You have a torch to light your way and a sacred amulet around your neck to protect you, so you know you are safe at all times. At the deepest point of the tunnel the path levels out into a clearing. You come upon a fire with a wise and ancient being seated before it. You may ask this being your question. Pay heed to the response, thank the being and return to the surface. You may return to seek out this wise being again whenever you have need of intuitive advice.

I am sometimes asked, 'Will talking about my intuition cause it to vanish?' The answer to this depends on the individual and the circumstance. In my experience if you have an intuitive idea for a creative work of some kind it is best not to speak about it before you have allowed the idea to fully develop or, if it has come to you complete, before you have had time to record it in an appropriate fashion. Intuition teaches you what you were previously unconscious of. To speak of this before you have fully brought the meaning to your own consciousness can dissipate it, as if by the act of making a list we feel we have already done the tasks we listed. You must learn to absorb the energy of such wisdom and hold it rather than diminish it by making it a conversational piece. The reason for reticence is that the act of explaining to anyone else involves evaluating and analysing the initial insight to find the right words and this will cause you to revert to the use of your rational mind. However brilliant you are at encapsulating the vision you will lose something in the process. Just as recording the details of a dream can never convey to anyone else how it was to experience the dream, the same is true of explanations.

An exception to this is the use of your workbook (see later in this chapter). You may quickly record the insight if you fear you cannot hold it in consciousness for long. Do not think about drawing perfectly or using words to impress. Scribble or sketch quickly so you do not lose the essence of the original intuition. If you can keep hold of the inner experience as you use the workbook it can serve as a bridge and the notes you make can evoke the original experience which otherwise might fade.

An instance when it may be appropriate to discuss your intuition is when it offers the solution to a specific problem and feels complete and utterly certain. You are amazed by its simplicity and truth. If you feel this intensity you are unlikely to forget the message, and the sharing of it with others is a sensible part of reality testing to check how viable the idea is. As with much to do with intuition you must rely on discrimination and experience to tell you when it is advisable and when not.

Techniques to develop Intuition

Now it is time to explore some ways to develop your intuition. As we have already realised, intuition may be enticed but cannot be commanded. Most of these techniques therefore involve becoming aware of habitual behaviour and thought patterns in order to change them or incorporate new ones. The aim is to make space for spontaneity. This may involve literally going to open spaces in nature where you will experience fewer distractions. Make the acceptance of intuition a new habit. Learn how to stop thinking, for a while, at least. It will enhance your receptivity to intuition. Allow yourself to experience emotions. The feeling qualities of immediacy, clarity and certainty which accompany intuitions cannot be explained or shared by anyone else, but can become familiar and trustworthy to you.

Not all of these techniques will suit your needs. The artist who wishes to tap into unconscious imagery is unlikely to choose the same technique as the employee who has to produce a presentation. But do try different techniques and be prepared to be playful. It may be the very fact of using unfamiliar materials which will free you from habitual thought patterns and allow your intuitive insights to surface. I will limit myself to a brief explanation of the many possibilities and suggest that you follow up any that appeal to you. Books, workshops, tapes and training are available for all these topics.

Relaxation

Relaxation, in its various forms, offers a rest from your thinking self. Learn to be, rather than to do. That may sound like a contradiction but you do not try to relax. There is no doing, just allowing, accepting and observing. Take some time out from your usual routines. Choose a place and time where you expect no interruptions, switch off telephones and find a comfortable place to sit. Sit rather than lie, since you will be more likely to sleep if you lie and while that is also beneficial it will not serve your intended purpose.

Take a deep breath and relax all the stress from your body. Identify any physical tensions with these simple exercises.

- Shrug your shoulders, raise them high and then drop them.
- Make fists of your hands and then relax them.
- Open your jaws wide and relax them.
- Frown and knit your browns tightly, then relax them.
- Flex your ankles then relax them.
- Curl your toes up tightly and then relax them.
- Slowly rotate your head on your shoulders. Repeat in the opposite direction.
- Take a deep breath and exhale slowly.
- Visualise the last time you were really happy.

Become aware of your body. Become aware of areas of tension or discomfort. Make yourself more comfortable. Notice your breathing without altering its rhythm by doing so. Imagine your breath flows to the site of any tension and smooths out the knots. Breathe naturally, merely observe. Notice your feelings without judgement and let them go. Allow yourself to experience whatever you feel but do not act on it. Remain calm and detached. If hoping for an intuitive breakthrough on a specific issue, do not think about it. You will merely repeat your usual thought patterns which have already failed you. Do not think about what happened yesterday, what you must do tomorrow, what remains to do today. If these things are important they will still be there. Just be with yourself and value the experience. Be here now. This state takes patience and practice. If you are normally a person who has to be rushing about, doing, or

planning to do, the art of being has to be learned. You may not gain an intuition immediately but you will have stirred the intuitive side of your brain. It may be that you will find ideas flow more freely later in the day, or it may take several sessions before you feel the benefit, but it *is* a habit worth cultivating.

The Workbook

It is extremely useful to keep a diary or workbook when you begin to develop your intuition as the accidental juxtapositions and happy jumble of your entries may inspire you. This is especially true if you have been in the habit of distrusting any but a reasoned and analytic approach to problem solving. This workbook will be a valuable resource for recapturing fleeting thoughts which will serve to show you with hindsight, how useful your insight has been and how you are developing a reliable and useful tool. You will have recorded the traceable pathways of your inspiration to allay doubts. Intending artists might also keep doodles and sketches, colour samples, ideas for designs in weaving, knitting, textile designs, jewellery and other creative endeavours in the workbook.

As you record and compare the results of intuitive experiments and experiences with previous examples, note which arose from the same kind of conditions and if you felt the same way when you experienced them. You will be mapping out your own intuitive territory and will then be better able to trust, or mistrust, what you take to be its landmarks. This is a necessary process until you become adept, because each person has a unique way of perceiving intuition, just as we each perceive all other aspects of the world around us in an individual way. There are no generalities which will fit every case.

Recording your experiences is important because intuitive experiences are marked by a particular feeling quality which you must come to recognise and trust. You will then be able to differentiate between intuitive feelings and wishful thinking with more confidence. Date the experience, dream or hunch so that you will not doubt yourself when

later it comes true. Did you start to doubt what had just seemed so certain? What are your feelings? Are you afraid of risk or of how to justify the actions prompted by the intuition? Note the outcome of any decisions to follow up on what you take to be intuition, and also of the results when you decide not to act. See if there is a pattern between the degree of importance and risk involved and your reluctance to act. By this means you will become more familiar with what intuition means to you, how you tend to receive it, and whether your ability to recognise it is improving, plus of course, whether the information gained was of value or not. Leave some space around your entries so that you can return to add later comments if necessary.

Intuitions may be in the form of dreams, perhaps when you were rarely aware of dreaming previously, or of sudden flashes of insight when relaxing or meditating, or when performing routine tasks which leave the mind free to meander. You may seem to hear an inner voice prompt you or have a firm emotional reaction of which you become aware but cannot explain. It may be that you will have a gut feeling or strong hunch. Tread carefully and expect to make over enthusiastic mistakes in reception and interpretation to start with, particularly if you have been a habitual rationalist. You will be as a stranger in a foreign land who conscientiously uses a phrase book, but speaks awkwardly when compared to a native speaker. You will miss many subtle nuances until fluency is gained, but if you are alert, you will know that you did miss them, and will thereby have increased your awareness for future occasions.

You may like to list the qualities which you believe an intuitive person will have. What makes an intuitive approach to a problem? Do you have any of these qualities? What changes would be required to behave in a similar way? Do you find the thought of such behaviour threatening? What precautions or reassurances would make the exploration of these qualities feel safe for you? Perhaps you might try them at home before doing so in the workplace. Perhaps keeping your attempts a secret will save embarrassment if you do not immediately succeed. Set up the conditions that allow you to play with new ways of approaching familiar activities. Even trivial changes can make a chink in the usual habitual armour.

Many artists know that to use a pencil or brush in the less favoured hand and to limit a sketch to a minute, or less, forces the normally judgemental mind to step aside. You may like to try this. There is simply no time for comparisons and use of the *wrong* hand gives less control over habitual marks on paper or canvas. What remains is hand and eye and the wisdom of intuitive seeing. If you find yourself cheating, set a timer. If your mind interferes, detach yourself from the thoughts and return to trusting hand and eye without the interference of thought. Let your mind glaze over as hand and eye work. No harm will come from setting control aside for a few minutes. You may be amazed with the results of this exercise, whether or not you consider yourself to be artistic.

You may try a similar exercise with poetry or prose. Allow a stream of consciousness to pass through your pen or typewriter without judgement or intervention for a set time limit. No one but you will see the results unless you choose to share it, so you need not fear inadequacy or ridicule. It may help to have one word as a *seed thought* to set you off, but thereafter write without considering the words. It may help to use the *wrong* hand, to emphasise freedom from usual restrictions. No matter if the result is almost illegible or full of spelling mistakes. If your mind starts to shape what you are writing, disconnect the thoughts and allow the thoughtless words to continue for the set period. Some writers use this technique to get them started when a blank page intimidates.

Try word associations, whether made in the form of a list, randomly on a page, or by using the *mind-mapping* technique. You can do this alone, using your workbook or artists materials, whatever is to hand and appropriate, or with other people with whom you brainstorm ideas.

- Write the keyword or words which relate to your problem. Now write down whatever word occurs to you by association with the first word(s) and then whatever word occurs to you from that, in a list of words. The ordered style of a list may prove repetitious enough to allow a spontaneous thought to surprise you.
- If you prefer, scatter words randomly on the page. Chance juxtapositions may help to trigger the insight you seek.

- Create a network of connections by linking each word with the one which triggered it in the style of *mind mapping,* (see Chapter 4). Make pathways of related words, starting a new one when the thought is at a tangent to those which went before.

The *mind-mapping* technique is a step further on from random or lists of free associations. You begin with your core idea and then enter the thoughts which are prompted by it, linking them where they seem to follow one from another, or starting a new pathway where they do not. It is a useful way of notetaking and the chance juxtapositions of keywords can sometimes trigger original connections.

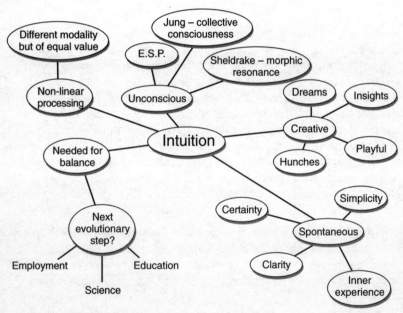

A sample mind map

To recap:

1 Keep a workbook.
2 Record experimental thoughts and ideas; doodles, sketches, colour samples, word associations, *mind maps*, dreams, sudden insights, inner voices, any repeated coincidences which you

notice, any strong emotional reactions towards or away from a stimulus, gut feelings, hunches.

3 Allow happy accidents to occur on the page. Do not attempt to be too ordered. It may be a chance juxtaposition which stirs creative vision.

4 Note any exercises, such as visualising or meditating, and the results which seem to flow from them.

5 Note when you decide to act on what you take to be an intuition and record the outcome.

6 Note when you decide not to act on what you take to be an intuition and the outcome.

7 Review the workbook periodically. It is easy to allow everyday life to close over us and so lose the direction our intuition was suggesting. It is also possible you will note the relevance of dreams and other phenomena only after some time has elapsed.

Creative Visualisation

Creative visualising or creative imagining can serve to free your thought processes by employing daydreaming in a loosely structured way. Make some time for creative day-dreaming. This unstructured thought can trigger intuitions. Choose a time when you will not be interrupted. You will get more from this exercise if you can manage twenty minutes or half an hour, because it takes a few minutes for the usual mind chatter to settle down. You may believe that you cannot visualise but if you have memories, you do it already. Try it: recollect the image of a much-loved place and imagine you experience the qualities which you find so pleasurable about being there. Do **not** recollect a particular memory of having been there in the past. Just take yourself in your mind to that location and be there now, in this moment. Give yourself a little time.

Alternatively, imagine a tranquil place. Take time to look about you. What can you smell, see, touch? Are you alone? Perhaps there are creatures or other people in the landscape? There is a seat nearby. Make yourself comfortable and feel the sunlight and a slight breeze upon your face. Remember the quiet place which you have created

within yourself. You can return to it whenever you need to tap into your creative imagination.

When you are experiencing the sense of being there you are visualising. When you wake is a good time to practice visualising. Your thinking faculties are suspended during sleep, so on waking, resistance to visualising and doubts about your ability to visualise will be less intrusive. Everyone can visualise to some degree.

Affirmations

> *We are what we think.*
> *All that we are arises with our thoughts.*
> *With our thoughts we create the world.*

The Buddha, quoted in *The Dhammapada*.

You may choose to employ affirmations to increase your focus on specific issues, or to attract certain aspects of consciousness. Mind can affect body. If you require convincing, try this well-known example:

> *Close your eyes and imagine you are holding a lemon to your nose. Imagine you can feel its nobbly texture and sense the oily waxiness of its skin. You can see its colour, size and texture in your mind's eye. Picture cutting the fruit. You can smell the sharp citrus scent. You squeeze a drop into your mouth and feel your tastebuds respond.*

By this point you will probably find you are salivating, although there is no real lemon present. A variation on this was the well-known schoolboy trick of sucking a real lemon in front of a brass band to the consternation of the players.

Thoughts and concepts are shaped by the language we use and we can actually programme ourselves by using positive thoughts and language. This can be as regular and conscious an activity as washing. As Pamela L. Travers' fictional character Mary Poppins was fond of saying, 'Everyday in every way I am getting better and

better': a well-known example of self-programming. Make your own affirmative statement, which must always be couched in positive language and should identify yourself, by name, with some event or quality which is within the realms of possibility, however distant that possibility may seem now. This could be. 'I ...., now free my intuition'. If you look at yourself in a mirror as you make your affirmation you help to reinforce its effect. Affirmations can also be done while in the calm state of relaxation, meditation or visualisation during which you may gently introduce a *seed thought*.

TAROT READINGS

The Tarot is an ancient form of divination using playing cards which convey the symbolism of many traditions. According to the way the cards are laid out these symbols can be interpreted to indicate current, past and future events. The use of tarot cards can thus externalise conscious and unconscious processes, since we interpret their meaning according to our inner prompting. I suggest that you learn the traditional meaning of the symbols depicted on the cards, and the basics of spreading them out, so that you can do your own readings. You can then try the tarot whenever you are at a loss for an answer or direction. There are numerous books which clearly lead you through the process. Though others may do a reading for you, their intuitions, while perhaps helpful for divination, will not necessarily prompt your intuitive reactions, as your own reactions to the symbols will.

I CHING

The I Ching, or Oracle of Change, is an ancient Chinese divination tool said to reflect the changes occurring at all levels in the universe and to act as a guide to your unconscious. It was the subject of much research by the psychologist Carl Jung. There are three methods of consulting the I Ching: The Yarrow Stalk, The Three Coins, and the

Six Wands method. The easiest of these for a western person may be the Three coins method but the best (and most complicated) is The Yarrow Stalks. I recommend that you employ a similar approach to that with the tarot for the purpose of nudging your intuition, and learn to make your own interpretations. There are many books on how to create and interpret a reading and although ideally one should use yarrow stalks, which may be hard to obtain, you can get a perfectly good reading using coins.

According to your chosen method, if you follow the instructions given, you obtain a series of numbers which, collected together, correspond to hexagrams. These hexagrams are symbolic representations of the relative positions of yin and yang energy (roughly speaking, passive and active energy) which resulted from casting the stalks, coins or wands and noting how they fell. By repeating this procedure a number of times you note enough hexagrams to make an interpretation. The hexagrams refer to specific interpretations which you look up, just as grid references lead you to a map site. The reading of these interpretations will supply the answer to the question you asked, or the situation generally prevailing at the time. These responses can be uncannily accurate reflections of the issues uppermost in your conscious mind and for this reason it is an excellent tool for nudging your unconscious and intuitive responses.

Biofeedback

Intuition is a natural human function which can be activated simply by removing the obstacles which our consciousness has erected. Biofeedback, a technique respected by many scientists because it is demonstrable and measurable, enables those who can learn to use it to remove those obstacles. Levels of consciousness can be scientifically registered by measuring brain waves, such as the delta waves which occur when we sleep. Biofeedback techniques involve learning to recognise how levels of consciousness feel and thereby being able to attain them at will.

When your brain enters a state of deep relaxation similar to that when almost asleep, alpha waves predominate. Theta waves are associated with even deeper states of relaxation and it is during these theta brain states that subjects report having dream-like visions. Inner imagery can be helped by contemplating an abstract idea because abstracts do not trigger specific visual connections which would then block new possibilities. For example, you might think of the abstract concept, weight. Not weight of…anything, just weight. If you try to hold the thought of weight you find a spontaneous image will occur. If trying to solve a problem relating to the design of a car you might hold the abstract thought, transport and see what comes to mind. If this is not the design aspect you need, perhaps the abstract, speed, would be more appropriate. There is an infinite number of abstract concepts you might use as a trigger factor.

Once you have had training in the biofeedback technique, find the abstract term which embraces the different aspects of the specific problem you have been working on, put your mind into a more receptive mode and then hold your abstract thought. New ideas and intuitions may be released.

(Meditation

Meditative techniques can be helpful in setting a relaxed tone suitable for allowing your intuitive wisdom. There are many ways to go about this but I recommend this simple technique if you have not tried it before. There is no need to adopt any particular posture, nor is it necessary to share any specific beliefs. This method can be practised by people of any faith or of none and of any physical ability.

1 **The time**   Pick a time when you should not be interrupted for at least twenty minutes. Switch off the telephone and ignore the doorbell if you can.

2 **The place**   The first requirement in meditating is that you feel relaxed. This may mean that you prefer to use a chair, a cushion on the floor, a bench in the park, a bed or wherever else you choose.

3 **The position**   The right position is whatever feels comfortable for you. Never mind the books on yoga, excellent though they can be. Meditation will work just as well without the lotus position, as with it. Lie or sit, but be aware that if you decide to lie down you may well drift into sleep rather than meditation. Sleep can also be beneficial, but unless it is dream sleep, it is unlikely to give access to your intuition.

4 **The ambiance**   Again, there is no need for special props. If you like the idea of incense or soothing background sounds, that is for you to decide. Normally I would recommend no props because you may come to rely on them, and then not always have them available when you want to meditate. However, if you cannot escape from a distractingly noisy environment, quietly playing recorded music may help you to feel that this is your personal sacred space, leaving the unwelcome noises beyond it, just as driving with the radio on can be calming.

5 **The method**   Make yourself comfortable in your chosen position. If you are paying attention to twinges or aching muscles you will be unable to let your mind drift. Calmly take a deep breath and exhale it when you are ready. This is not a test of how deep a breath you can take nor how long you can hold it. A lot of tension is held in the neck and shoulders so you may like to gently allow your head to roll around on your neck. Shrug your shoulders a few times, bringing them up towards your ears before relaxing them.

Be still and aware, without thinking. If a thought enters your mind, as it surely will, observe it and let it go. Do not lose patience with yourself. If you notice thoughts have stopped, that is another thought, let that go too. Learn to be like a cat at a mousehole; patient, relaxed, but all attention. Intuitions may flash into the stillness.

Dreams

Dreams represent a valuable access to the preconscious levels of the mind. Scientists assure us that we do all dream, though we may not

be aware of having done so. As the track record of intuitive breakthroughs in science, the arts and mathematics attest, dreams have often provided a precise answer to a problem, a complete poem or an inspiration for a complete piece of music.

You can increase your awareness of dreams by being prepared to honour them. By this I mean act as though you expect to dream and you will be rewarded. If not successful at the first attempt, do persevere. I have known of many instances of people who thought they did not dream, only to find that they became the most prolific dreamers once their unconscious mind knew it had an audience. I confess I was one such, and now I possess full dream diaries spanning more than fifteen years.

- Prepare to record dreams by placing pen and paper, or a cassette recorder near where you will sleep, together with access to a light in case you wake up in the middle of the night.
- Silently ask your mind for a dream before sleeping. This autosuggestion does help, so do not dismiss it until you have tried it a few times. You can use the same trick to waken at a set time when you have no alarm clock.
- Allow yourself a healthy sleep not exhausted by overwork, or dulled by too much food or alcohol.
- If seeking the answer to a specific problem, ask to be shown the answer. This is not as fanciful as it may seem. You may need to return to an item of a former dream that you did not understand. Ask for a second dream to give you clarity.

The dreaming mind operates in imaginal, pictorial and non-sequential ways, matching feelings with objects in a way that would rarely, if ever occur to us when awake. This form of information processing can thus become the source of intuitive wisdom if we record our dreams. They are not language dependent or ordered by the usual limitations of time and space. Dreams are the stories that we tell ourselves, related in a symbolic language. As a result dreams have been dismissed by some people as little more than mental static. However, dreams are not nonsensical once we learn to decipher them. They sometimes represent the reworking of our conscious issues, so if we take them seriously, we may find the answers we seek. We need to respect and honour them in the same

way that we must treat intuition, if we want to benefit from their wisdom.

The first step towards understanding your dreams is to record them. It is important that you record the dream as soon as you wake up. If you think to yourself that you will do so later in the day, or you decide to go back to sleep intending to record it when you wake again, you can be sure that you will distort, if not lose parts or all the dream entirely. These are the important aspects to jot down while the feeling and memory is still with you.

- Record the dream narrative; the story, if there was one.
- Make a note of what seemed to be the most important element of the dream.
- What was your role in the dream? Were you an invisible witness or could you observe yourself as an active participant?
- Note the point in the dream when you awoke, what was about to happen and how you felt about it.
- Note how you felt on waking. This may be happy, sad, afraid, excited, certain, in fact any of the emotions of which we are capable. You may be able to release an emotion through the safety of a dream that you feel you cannot when awake.
- If you seek intuitional advice, this may come in the form of a definite revelation, the precise answer to a specific question, but it may be more oblique. Record the dream so that you may understand it later.

Interpreting your dreams is a skill you should develop rather than relying on reference books, as helpful as these can be in some circumstances. Dream reference books may sometimes be useful, for instance when an image has a universal meaning of which you were not aware, but even if such a meaning exists, you must feel that it fits in your case. Each element in a dream has personal meaning, because it was produced, written and directed by your mind using the references available to you. This is so even when the images seem chaotically bizarre, since they pictorially represent feelings and many of these may not be consciously acknowledged at all. As we are only considering dream interpretation for its relevance to intuition we cannot go into too much detail here.

If you begin to be aware of your dreams for the first time you may find some aspects disturbing. I will therefore mention a few elements which are commonly misunderstood.

- Remember all the elements are merely symbols which stand in for aspects of your own life. They mirror your feelings and rarely represent scenes of what is actually happening in the present or what may really happen in the future.
- A known person in a dream is more likely to represent the qualities which you associate with them, rather than mean you are a secret witness to the activities of that real person.
- A death is almost never an indication of death; rather it symbolically suggests impending change since, for the new to be born, the old must die. This could be something abstract such as an idea, a habit, an emotion or an attitude, just as much as a change to material objects or situations.

- Violence committed by you, or towards you, is most likely to be an indication of the depth of your feelings or perceptions concerning a current situation and is not in any sense an indication or portent of real violence. It can be taken as a hint to examine how honest you are being with yourself in relation to this issue, since the conflict suggests deeper feelings than are being expressed in your waking life.
- Learn to decipher your own dream symbols. While dream dictionaries may give a general interpretation, you have personal and unique associations with the contents of your mind, so your meaning may be different. Go with the version that feels right to you. If you have to intellectualise the interpretation you have not found the answer. Record the meanings you ascribe to dream symbols and build up your own dictionary.

A WORD OF WARNING

Respect the flow of your intuition and record it if you do not want it to be lost. It will rarely be accessible to you again. Remember the

cautionary tale of 'The person on business from Porlock' who interrupted Coleridge and detained him for more than an hour when he had been recording an intuitive flow of verse, the epic poem *Kubla Khan*. According to Coleridge, following a chance prompt and having taken prescribed medicine (possibly opium), he fell into a reverie. The verses flowed fully formed to his mind and were recorded by him as fast as he could write. Then came disaster. A knock at the door disturbed him and interrupted the verse. It was a person from the village of Porlock on a matter of business. When Coleridge returned to his pen the connection with his intuition was lost to him. So the epic poem remains unfinished, and the person from Porlock, whoever he was, entered into legend with Coleridge's bitter description of the incident.

Coleridge's example is a reminder that intuition is fleeting and so demands your immediate and complete attention. Too easily it will dissipate before you can get a conscious hold on it even though you may think that you could never forget such a gem, that you will remember it in the morning, or that you will write it down when you get home: be warned. Your habitual ways of thinking will have taken over again and the full clarity of the intuitive realisation will have been contaminated or lost.

PRACTICE

1 How is surrender relevant to intuition?
2 Make it a routine to write something in your workbook daily, however brief and however irrelevant it may seem. It cements a contract with your unconscious that it will be accorded respect.
3 Are scenes involving dream characters to be taken literally?
4 What does the story of 'The person from Porlock' teach us?

7

INTUITION AT WORK

*...organisational effectiveness does not lie in that narrow-minded concept called 'rationality'; it lies in a blend of clear-headed logic **and** powerful intuition.*

Henry Mintzberg, *Harvard Business Review*, July/August 1976

The wider context

The wider acceptance of intuition as a valuable resource has global implications, since though we tend to think of ourselves as unique and separate, the changes we make as individuals affect those around us. Those whom we affect then affect others with whom they are in contact, and so influence spreads ever outward. If we want to make a difference, we must start with ourselves and how we work. The parochial can become global.

Intuition in the workplace

Good management does not rely on facts alone. If that is all it takes, every company with the same facts should be equal. What marks the difference between the successful and unsuccessful company, given equal resources, is the use to which information is put, and that depends upon individual flair and a degree of intuition. Most western businesses favour thinking over intuiting, except those

involved with the arts, media and advertising. In his autobiography *Be my guest* (1957), Conrad Hilton, founder of the worldwide hotel chain, tells of his reliance on intuition. It was a hunch that got Hilton into the hotel business and intuition which prompted him to make the right bids when taking over other properties. He says, 'I think the other name for hunch is intuition…But the key to intuition is not in the prayer but in listening for a response.'

The ability to recognise insights and the courage to follow hunches is a necessary skill in management, particularly when a situation presents us with an enormous amount of complex detail. The amount of analytic evaluation required in such situations can be more than a rationally thinking manager, however good his or her reasoning powers, could usefully evaluate. It even takes a certain capacity for holistic thinking to know which raw data would be more usefully calculated using a computer. Without an ability to sense trends and judge the wider situation, facts fed into a computer may be useless for extracting meaningful information, however fast the operating speed of the machine. The whole is thus greater than the sum of the parts.

Since complex problems are more effectively dealt with by holistic thinking, if we hold loose guidelines for achieving goals, we then allow space for intuition. Rigid approaches to a problem will only repeat what is already known and since there is a problem, that is obviously not enough. It takes someone with the ability to assume a broad overview to give a company the advantage over those relying merely on factual knowledge. Here are some tips:

- Encourage some flights of fancy in planning meetings.
- Be protective of ideas, however crazy they seem initially.
- Allow ambiguities and speculations.
- Avoid using your rank or status to intimidate.
- Avoid censure and ridicule. If staff feel uncertain about making contributions because of the possible repercussions, you may lose their valuable ideas.
- Keep all options loose. There will be time for evaluation before implementation.
- Ask team members to dream up as many solutions to the problem as they can, no matter how wild.

- Make the freedom to explore ideas safe and explicit. The harvest from intuitive sessions such as this may provide the direction you seek.

Employ staff effectively

The effective manager will know who is an intuitive type and who favours routine and repetitive work. While each type can be encouraged to use other aspects of their capacities, it makes sense to put the right person to work in the right area. The intuitive person would do well in forward planning, where creative vision and a flair for sensing trends are at a premium. The thinking type would more usefully be employed where data is to be manipulated and maintained, where detail and precision are paramount. Such people will draw on experience and meet targets.

Intuition in Education

Educationists would do well to encourage the skills of research, listening, communication, understanding and recall rather than learning facts by rote. There is a tendency to think that what *we* know is what is. We expect children to exactly reproduce the same things that we learned, but if we encouraged originality and creativity, we might be the ones to learn and our children might be the scientists and innovators of tomorrow. Teaching should combine awareness of the facts and achievements attained so far in a subject, together with the skills of research and experimentation which will form the basis of creative work in the future. The fusion of history and technique within eager minds encouraged to seek, rather than absorb, is the way for science and society to progress. All too often creative and intuitive work is dismissed as irrelevant by a system geared to reproducing identical intellectual clones.

There exists an almost transcendent reality over and above any collection of component parts, or facts, of which the effective teacher will be aware. The dissection of a frog into all its parts, even down to the cells of which its body is composed will give you little idea of what a frog is, it's *frogness*, if you had never seen a live one. So lists of all known facts relating to a subject to be learned, will not reveal the deeper level of truth. It is like the learning of a language. We may learn vocabulary, verbs and the rules of grammar by rote, but it is not until we bring them to life within us by formulating our own speech that we truly learn the language.

We should encourage children to value intuition and analysis, not create the situation where analysis is seen as the only way to solve problems and intuition is impractical. To develop a receptivity to intuition means removing the blocks which prevent us from receiving it. Young children have few, but as we grow older we learn that intuition is not quite respectable and become fixed in our ways of thinking. We learn to base judgements on past experience rather than risk anything new.

Achievable goals and metagoals

The prime objective of any task or problem can be defined, but can also be evaluated and broken into the smaller goals which would be necessary steps on the way to the grand goal. The act of reducing the major goal allows achievable aims to become a daily habit, which then leads to personal satisfaction when mini goals are reached and encourages a continual, spiral movement towards the grand goal. Considered in its entirety the grand goal may seem too daunting. The smaller steps enable us to overcome fear and inertia. The journey of a thousand miles must begin with the first step.

Within a company situation you may:

1 Collectively debate, determine and agree on the desired goal(s). Do not be tempted into offering solutions at this stage.

Encourage wild ideas and avoid prejudegment. It is easier to tame than to inspire.

2 Encourage individual effort toward achieving this goal, each person employing their own, unique, approach to the issue within a broadly supportive and encouraging environment. This is more productive than a collective brainstorming of ideas. They can be intimidating to introverted colleagues or may always be dominated by the most extroverted, though not necessarily the most creative, members of the team.

3 Arrange for the collection of individual contributions in a stress-free and non-judgemental environment. This may mean one-to-one exchanges of ideas, small group meetings which may provoke insights from other team members and useful cross-fertilisation of ideas, or by the submission of private reports.

4 Reappraise the results so far. Team leaders must assess intuitive material for its suitability for the project, goal or vision and determine what would be required as a result of the ideas suggested to make them happen. Sorting out the practicalities may reveal new goals not apparent at stage one.

5 Enact the proposed changes and monitor results.

6 Review and reassess.

7 Return to 1 above with the new insights, goals and projects which arose as a result of reaching the new vantage point. Avoid closure. Achievement involves a dynamic and ever turning spiral. With each goal comes a new challenge to take the subject yet further. There is never a point in business where we can sit back and think, 'that's it'.

The future of intuition

It is time to revalue the non-rational gifts we are blessed with. Changes in core thinking like *fuzzy logic* make new processes and inventions possible and make us aware there are different ways of interpreting old problems. The time is ripe for intuition to be reassessed and recognised as a valuable element in creativity, decision making and problem solving.

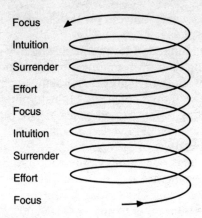

Focus
Intuition
Surrender
Effort
Focus
Intuition
Surrender
Effort
Focus

Creativity and intuition

PRACTICE

1 How might you incorporate intuitional processes into your working life?
2 What is your primary goal? How could this be broken into smaller elements?
3 How might you use your intuition to tackle the more manageable goals?
4 Why choose a spiral as a model for the intuitive process?

ENDPIECE
WHY NOW?

Discovery consists of seeing what everybody has seen and thinking what nobody has thought.

Albert Szent-Györgi (1893–1986), Biochemist who isolated vitamin C

So why should we value intuition now? Carl Jung believed that the western world generally favours the thinking processes and as a consequence, neglects the feeling processes. The eastern world, he said, tends to favour the opposite. This has global implications in a world where the scientific discoveries of the west can enhance or destroy us all.

Jung foresaw the revaluing of intuition in the west as an important means of balancing unchecked reason. Though the psychological type which we favour predisposes us to use this function and resist its opposite, the dormant quality is not lost to us forever. It can be encouraged to respond at conscious levels and we can even out our modes of thinking. You need not sacrifice any of your reasoning skills or rational capabilities in order to enhance your intuition and feelings, any more than you would have to sacrifice your intuition if you wanted to develop your powers of reason. The development of the *lost* faculty makes for a more balanced human being, not a diminished one.

Science is important but it, too, relies on intuitive input to progress. We learn of the end product of previous intuitive successes, once they have been evaluated and passed into common use and knowledge and forget the means by which they were discovered.

Albert Einstein for instance was fascinated in his youth by the properties of light. He is reported to have daydreamed as a young man that he rode on a beam of light back to its origin. He had the faith to trust his vision rather than ignore it, and devoted the next several years to trying to prove mathematically what he had seen with his mind's eye. As Einstein said, 'The intellect has little to do on the road to discovery. There comes a leap in consciousness, call it intuition or what you will, and the solution comes to you and you don't know how or why.'

How can we expect succeeding generations to be similarly creative if all they are told is of the end product and not the processes by which it was arrived at? No amount of methodical sifting of facts will produce new ways of problem solving unless synthesised by insight into an intuitive breakthrough. How many other intuitive revelations were lost because their recipient lacked Einstein's courage to pursue them? The balance to be gained by adding intuitive wisdom to the already well developed skills of reason might even be said to be our next evolutionary task, if we are to avoid the excesses that advances in science could bring us.

Intuition responds to the general context of a question so that imaginative and creative connections can be made which our rational, linear thought patterns would be unlikely to make. It is as if every conscious thought and idea occupies a fixed point, but these points rest on a backdrop of much greater, perhaps limitless, unconscious potential; of a virtual network of perpetual possibilities; of ever possible becomings. Thus intuition cannot be limited to linking only consciously known points. Once we have set the agenda with our conscious interest, intuition connects the possibilities of which we are not aware. Focusing upon the problem with our conscious effort seems to draw forward from infinite possibility, those connections with relevance for our context, as if the connections resonate to the same note, or respond to the same frequency. The resulting intuition may suggest new combinations never before juxtaposed by anyone, as with the creation of a poem, or the discovery of a cure for a disease. For instance I wonder what was the trigger for deciding that the double helix is the correct model of the DNA molecule. Might it have been a long forgotten sight of a twisted Elizabethan chimney stack, a stick of

barley sugar candy, or the way wool and rope is plied from many strands? A mind in free association can make reference to items from completely different registers than those likely to be made by a rationally ordered mind. We will never know what the reference points were for DNA, just as we will not know which routers have passed and forwarded the parts of our *Internet* message. All we know is that they arrive, when they do.

Must we care how intuition works, if we can convince ourselves that it does? Perhaps one day explanations will be found, but just because intuition operates beyond our conscious will and has defied neat definitions, does not give adequate grounds for dismissing it along with occult phenomena. We accept a good deal of science on no better a basis. Intuition represents a level of awareness or consciousness available to all, but seldom used. So long as it works and is of benefit, perhaps that is of no importance. A willingness to learn from intuition is a willingness to learn the truth. If you develop your awareness of intuition and maximise the reliability of this skill you will be well rewarded. Once you are clear about how and when you experience intuition and can discriminate it from mere wishing or daydreaming you will come to value intuition as one of the most practical and natural of your abilities. It will never replace the need for rational evaluation and critical judgement, but it can increase your sense of what is possible and be the means to make your own luck.

fURThER REAOING

Betty Bethards, *The Dream Book*, Inner Light Foundation, California, 1983

Tony Buzan and Terence Dixon, *The Evolving Brain*, David and Charles Ltd, UK, 1978

Brian Cooper (Ed), *The Internet*, Dorling Kindersley Ltd, London, 1996

B. Ghiselin (Ed), *The Creative Process*, University of California Press, Los Angeles and London, 1985

Philip Goldberg, *The Intuitive Edge*, Turnstone Press, UK, 1989

E. Hutchinson, *How to think creatively*, Abingdon-Cokesbury, New York, 1949

John R. Levine, Carol Baroudi & Margaret L. Young, *The Internet for Dummies*, 4th edition, IDG Books Worldwide, Inc., 1997

Henry Mintzberg, 'Planning on the Left side and Managing on the Right', *Harvard Business Review*, July/August, 1976

Plato, Trans. by Desmond Lee, *The Republic*, Penguin Classics, 1987

Howard Rheingold, *Virtual Reality*, Secker & Warburg, 1991

Kevin J. Todeschi, *The Encyclopedia of Symbolism*, A Perigree Book, New York, 1995

Geoffrey Underwood and Robin Stevens (Eds), *Aspects of Consciousness Volume 1: Psychological Issues*, Academic Press Inc. (London) Ltd, 1979

Joseph Weizenbaum, *Computer power and human reason*, W.H. Freeman & Co, 1976: Penguin Books, 1993

The Hodder & Stoughton beginner's guides series includes the following titles which may be of interest: *Dream Interpretation*; *I Ching*; *Interpreting Signs and Symbols*; *Meditation*; *Tarot*; *Visualisation*; *Becoming Prosperous*.